Fall color on the Deschutes River, Route 32

Lava rock outcroppings make for technical winter riding at Radlands, Route 2.

The Ochoco Mountains promise ripping-fun trails, such as Cougar Creek, Route 39. (Photo: Travis Holman)

A rider navigates rocky goodness in the Ochoco Mountains on the Cougar Creek Trail, Route 39. (Photo: Travis Holman)

Downhill shredders wait for the lift ride at Mount Bachelor Bike Park, Route 22.

*Wide-open juniper and sage country at Grasslands,
Route 4* (Photo: Chris Kratsch)

*The Peterson Ridge trails, Route 40, offer close-up
views of the Three Sisters.* (Photo: Chris Kratsch)

Smith Rock State Park, Route 3, serves up sublime views of the Crooked River and popular rock climbing crags such as the Monkey Face spire.

Next page: *The cool, lush, and green McKenzie River Trail, Route 44* (Photo: Melanie Fisher)

MOUNTAIN
BIKE
BEND

46 SELECT
SINGLETRACK
ROUTES

KATY BRYCE

MOUNTAINEERS
BOOKS

For Chris
"I got this."

MOUNTAINEERS
BOOKS

Mountaineers Books is the publishing division of The Mountaineers, an organization founded in 1906 and dedicated to the exploration, preservation, and enjoyment of outdoor and wilderness areas.

1001 SW Klickitat Way, Suite 201, Seattle, WA 98134
800.553.4453, www.mountaineersbooks.org

Printed in the United States of America
Distributed in the United Kingdom by Cordee, www.cordee.co.uk
First edition, 2017

Copyeditor: Erin Moore
Design: Jen Grable
Layout: Peggy Egerdahl
Cartographer: Pease Press Cartography
Cover photograph: *Mountain biking in the Ochoco Mountains* (Photo: Troy McMullin / Pacific Crest Stock)
Back cover photograph: *The Wanoga trail network is one of many fantastic riding areas near Bend.* (Photo: Cog Wild)
All photos by Katy Bryce, unless noted otherwise.

The background maps for this book were produced using the online map viewer CalTopo. For more information, visit www.caltopo.com.

Library of Congress Cataloging-in-Publication Data
Names: Bryce, Katy.
Title: Mountain bike, Bend : 46 select singletrack routes / Katy Bryce.
Description: Seattle, WA : Mountaineers Books, [2017] | Includes index.
Identifiers: LCCN 2016046431 (print) | LCCN 2017003083 (ebook) | ISBN 9781680510645 (trade paper) | ISBN 9781680510652 (ebook)
Subjects: LCSH: Mountain biking—Oregon—Bend—Guidebooks. | Trails—Oregon—Bend—Guidebooks. | Bend (Or.)—Guidebooks.
Classification: LCC GV1045.5.O72 B463 2017 (print) | LCC GV1045.5.O72 (ebook) | DDC 796.6309795/87—dc23
LC record available at https://lccn.loc.gov/2016046431

Mountaineers Books titles may be purchased for corporate, educational, or other promotional sales, and our authors are available for a wide range of events. For information on special discounts or booking an author, contact our customer service at 800-553-4453 or mbooks@mountaineersbooks.org.

♻ Printed on recycled paper

ISBN (paperback): 978-1-68051-064-5
ISBN (ebook): 978-1-68051-065-2

CONTENTS

NORTH OF BEND   37

WEST OF BEND AND WANOGA   55

WALDO LAKE   **119**

EAST AND SOUTH OF BEND   **141**

CROOK COUNTY AND OCHOCO MOUNTAINS   **163**

SISTERS 181

McKENZIE RIVER 197

ROUTES AT A GLANCE

	Route	Mileage	Ride Type	Technical Difficulty	Fitness Intensity
1.	The Maston	11.6	Network	Beginner–intermediate	Easy
2.	Radlands	Up to 9	Network	Advanced	Easy
3.	Smith Rock	12.1	Loop	Advanced	Strenuous
4.	Grasslands	9.3	Loop	Advanced	Moderate
5.	Otter Bench	6.8	Out-and-back	Advanced	Moderate
6.	Phil's Canyon	16.2	Loop	Intermediate	Moderate
7.	Kent's and COD	20.8	Loop	Advanced	Strenuous
8.	COD and Grand Slam	20.7	Loop	Advanced	Strenuous
9.	Tumalo Falls and Whoops	17	Out-and-back	Intermediate	Moderate
10.	Mrazek	32.2	Out-and-back	Intermediate	Moderate–very strenuous
11.	Funner and Tiddlywinks	23.9	Loop	Intermediate	Strenuous
12.	Tyler's Traverse	12.8	Loop	Intermediate	Strenuous
13.	Wanoga to Dinah-Moe-Humm	21	Out-and-back	Advanced	Strenuous
14.	Dutchman to Flagline to Phil's	22.1	Shuttle	Advanced	Strenuous
15.	Dutchman to Metolius–Windigo to Shevlin Park	25.6	Shuttle	Advanced	Strenuous
16.	Swede Ridge and South Fork	13.3	Loop	Advanced	Moderate
17.	North Fork and Farewell	16.6	Loop	Advanced	Strenuous
18.	Swampy Lakes and Vista Butte	8.1	Loop	Intermediate	Moderate
19.	North Fork, Metolius–Windigo, and South Fork	24.5	Loop	Advanced	Very strenuous
20.	Ride Around Mount Bachelor	31.2	Loop	Advanced–expert	Very strenuous
21.	Lava Lake to Sparks Lake	25.6	Out-and-back	Advanced	Strenuous

	Route	Mileage	Ride Type	Technical Difficulty	Fitness Intensity
22.	Mount Bachelor Bike Park	Up to 15	Network	Intermediate–expert	Easy–strenuous
23.	Waldo Lake Trail	20.2	Loop	Advanced	Strenuous
24.	Lemish and Charlton Lakes	18	Loop	Advanced	Strenuous
25.	Cultus Lake	11.7	Loop	Beginner	Moderate
26.	The Twins	19	Loop	Advanced	Strenuous
27.	Maiden Peak	12.2	Out-and-back	Advanced	Very strenuous
28.	Mount Ray and Fuji Mountain	14.3	Loop	Advanced	Strenuous
29.	Horse Ridge	12.0	Loop	Advanced	Moderate
30.	Horse Butte	12.8	Loop	Intermediate	Moderate
31.	Swamp Wells	26	Loop	Intermediate	Strenuous
32.	Deschutes River Trail	23	Out-and-back	Intermediate	Easy–strenuous
33.	Black Rock Trail	8.2	Out-and-back	Beginner	Easy
34.	Newberry Caldera	22.6	Loop	Advanced	Very strenuous
35.	Lower 66	Up to 2.5	Network	Intermediate	Easy
36.	Lookout Mountain	18.5	Loop	Advanced–expert	Very strenuous
37.	Round and Lookout Mountains Epic	28.7	Loop	Advanced–expert	Very strenuous
38.	Independent Mine	8.7	Loop	Intermediate	Moderate
39.	Cougar Creek	15.8	Out-and-back	Advanced	Strenuous
40.	Peterson Ridge	Up to 25	Network	Intermediate–advanced	Moderate
41.	Cache Mountain	12	Loop	Advanced	Strenuous
42.	Trail 99	13.2	Shuttle	Advanced	Moderate
43.	Suttle Tie to Suttle Lake	13.7	Out-and-back	Beginner	Easy
44.	McKenzie River Trail	24.9	Shuttle	Advanced	Strenuous
45.	King Castle to Castle Rock	13.2	Out-and-back	Advanced	Strenuous
46.	Olallie and O'Leary Epic	27.8	Loop	Expert	Very strenuous

ACKNOWLEDGMENTS

The fun I had researching and writing this book would have never been possible without the hundreds of Oregon trail builders and maintainers, mostly volunteers, who work endless hours to create some of the best mountain bike trails in the country. My husband, Chris, was instrumental in helping me with this book, and my friends and fellow mountain bikers also deserve double high-fives for riding with me even when it meant stopping frequently for a photo op or to look at the map. This book is yours, too.

RIDE LOCATOR MAP

INTRODUCTION

My first mountain bike was a 1995 steel, hardtail Gary Fisher that fit me poorly, shifted sluggishly, and was as heavy as a ship anchor. Yet that mountain bike became my ticket to freedom, adventure, friendships, and a lifetime of challenges, both physical and mental. After I moved to Bend, Oregon, in 1997, my first serious mountain bike ride was a third of the way up Phil's Canyon—a mere 4 miles—though at the time it seemed much farther. In my cheap bike shorts and tennis shoes, I pedaled up the dry canyon, thinking that I was "really out there." With no cell phone or GPS device, it was just me alone in the woods, hoping I would make it home.

Oh, how things have changed! Twenty years later, on my ultralight, full-suspension carbon mountain bike, riding is a wonderfully different experience. The mountain biking trails in and around Bend have exploded both in quantity and quality, and we now have hundreds of miles to ride. From family-friendly cruiser trails that start right in Bend, to lift-accessed downhill screamers and high-elevation rides far from civilization, there is something for everyone. Bend, Oregon, is a near-perfect place for mountain biking.

I feel fortunate to have experienced the wide variety of trails all within a two-hour drive from one of the best towns in the Pacific Northwest. Here, you can bag a 50-mile-long, all-singletrack mountain bike ride during the day, then sip on one of our award-winning craft brews at night. As much as I love to travel to faraway places, I'm always happy to come home to beautiful Bend and pedal my way across the heart of Oregon.

Opposite: *Riders take in a view of Mount Bachelor in the High Cascades.*
(Photo: Cog Wild)

With *Mountain Bike: Bend,* I can share that experience and my favorite rides with you. The rides in this guidebook are easily accessed from Bend, and they reflect a beautiful and diverse region, from the hot, dry high desert east of town to the cool, moist old-growth forests to the west. You might notice that Oakridge trails are not included in this guide. That is simply because there are so many trails in the Oakridge area, and many more that are currently being planned and built, that it deserves its own guide.

OVERVIEW OF BEND AND SURROUNDING AREAS

Oregon is divided geographically by the Cascade Range, which runs north–south from northern Washington to northern California and is marked by volcanic peaks reaching upward of 11,000 feet. East of the Cascade crest, the slopes descend gradually until they reach Bend, where the Deschutes River cuts through the high desert. West of the Cascade crest, the hills drop steeply, carved by deep valleys such as the McKenzie River valley.

The Cascades give the area a dramatic ecological diversity, too. The high desert around Bend, in the rain shadow of the Cascades, is dominated by sagebrush and western juniper (Routes 1–5, 29, and 30), which changes to dry ponderosa pine forest (Routes 6–13) and morphs still higher into a mix of hemlocks, firs, spruces, and high-elevation pines (Routes 14–28). Descending back down the wetter west side of the mountains, the plant life transforms again into ultragreen, moss-covered forest. The McKenzie River trails (Routes 44–46) showcase this type of classic Oregon forest.

East of Bend, near the community of Prineville, are the older, more weathered Ochoco Mountains with their distinct vegetation (see Routes 35–39). And southeast of Bend lies Newberry Volcano (Route 34), which is actually part of the Cascade Range even though it sits to the east of the rest of the peaks.

The primary river flowing through central Oregon is the Deschutes, which originates from Little Lava Lake (Routes 20 and 21), then turns north to flow all the way to the Columbia River. On its way north, the Deschutes passes through open sage country near Redmond and Terrebonne, where it converges with the Crooked River, which carved the amazing Smith Rock into its dramatic geologic display (Routes 3 and 4).

HOW TRAILS ARE BUILT AND MAINTAINED

"Trails don't build themselves" is something you often hear in these parts. While all of the rides listed in this guidebook are on public lands managed, for example, by the US Forest Service or Bureau of Land Management, those

Riders take a break on the Deschutes River Trail, Route 32.

land management agencies often rely on volunteers to build and maintain trails. As public lands shift toward more recreation, and away from logging and extraction, many of the agencies are partnering closely with local trail organizations to steward the trails.

In the greater Bend area, on public lands east of the Cascade crest, the Central Oregon Trail Alliance (COTA) is the driving force behind building and maintaining mountain bike trails, with four chapters representing Bend, Sisters, Redmond, and Crook County. The all-volunteer COTA is truly a force for good. Armed with shovels, Pulaskis, chain saws, and motorized trail building machinery, they log thousands of volunteer hours each year and host trail work events of all sizes, including Spring Fling and Biketoberfest. These biannual community events draw hundreds of mountain biking enthusiasts together to "dirt scratch" and make their favorite trails even better. COTA is largely supported and funded through local business sponsorships, individual memberships, and the occasional grant. I highly recommend supporting COTA with your volunteer time or a paid membership—or both! Visit www .cotamtb.com to learn more and become a member.

The Sisters Trails Alliance (STA; www.sisterstrails.com) is another, smaller organization that stewards the Peterson Ridge trails and other trails in the Sisters region. Trails in the Willamette National Forest, including those in the Waldo Lake area and in the McKenzie River valley, receive love and attention from two other prominent trail organizations in greater Oregon: the Eugene-based Disciples of Dirt (DOD; www.disciplesofdirt.org) and the Oakridge-based Greater Oakridge Area Trail Stewards (GOATS; www.oakridgegoats.org). Staff and volunteers with these organizations spend countless hours constructing and building trails. They could use your help, too.

Thanks to these organizations, new trails are built and old trails are revived every year. In fact, several trails were in planning or ready-to-build stages as I researched and wrote this guidebook, and I've included notes about new trails and reroutes in the appropriate ride write-ups.

THE BIRTH OF BEND MOUNTAIN BIKING

Central Oregon has a rich history of cycling and mountain biking. While riders in Marin County, California, were modifying cruiser bikes to ride down Mount Tam in the 1970s, a group of road riders here in Bend were also forging their way in what would become one of the best-known riding areas in the country. A pivotal moment came in 1979 when intrepid cyclists Gary Bonacker (currently part owner of Bend's Sunnyside Sports), Tim Boyle, and Don Ipock descended Mount Bachelor on their own "klunkers," the name given to the early bikes that were slightly modified to withstand riding on dirt. After their wild ride down the mountain, local interest in off-road cycling surged.

Adventurous cyclists started converting their Schwinns to three-speed shifting and adding cantilever brakes. In 1981, Bend resident and cyclist Bob Woodward traveled to Marin County to converge with mountain bike legends Gary Fisher, Charlie Kelly, and Tom Ritchey at their new "mountain bike" company in Marin. Soon after returning to Bend, Woodward wrote a story about the trip for an outdoor trade magazine, spurring even greater national and local interest in this new outdoor activity—and in Bend as a place to do it. Woodward would later become mayor of Bend in the late 1990s.

From there, two camps of riders developed around Bend: road cyclists, including Bonacker, Woodward, and Dennis Oliphant, and off-road motorcyclists, including Dennis Heater (of Heater Rock fame at the top of Phil's Canyon) and Brad Stankey, who produced the locally made Outback Bikes. Heater was known as the king of mountain bike fun and was always organizing cruiser crawls, poker rides, overnighters, and epic one-day rides like the "Big Hair—No Brains" rides.

COTA volunteers build a new section of COD in the Phil's Trail network, Routes 7 and 8.

Heater and Phil Meglasson (the "Phil" of Phil's Trail) started working on creating new trails. In 1989, after professional mountain biker Paul Thomasberg moved to town, Bend took off as a mountain bike destination.

Woodward is well known in Bend for sharing vintage photos and early Bend mountain biking lore. I talked with Woodward in April 2016, and he shared the following: "We first rode old logging doubletrack roads and soon started linking them together with sections of singletrack. One Saturday in 1983 or 1984, I was going along an old doubletrack when I saw a game trail, so I followed it and it came out a mile or so later at another old road. That Sunday, Phil and I went out and brushed the game trail. Weeks later, Jim Terhaar sketched in a new trail past the second road. Then Paul Thomasberg added some trail and Jeff Frizzle even more. It was the start of the Phil's Trail system."

And the rest, as they say, is history. These historic trails, in addition to new trails, are now enjoyed by thousands of mountain bikers each year.

King Castle Trail, Route 45, has fun and fast switchbacks.

KNOW BEFORE YOU GO

Flying through the trees and over sharp lava rock at high speed is inherently dangerous, but it is also part of the thrill of mountain biking. Riding a mountain bike has its risks, and anything can happen—some of my worst crashes have resulted from rolling over innocent-looking pinecones. Fortunately, many of the risks can be mitigated and your trip enjoyment maximized through good preparation and a solid understanding of what you are getting into when you set out on a ride. From having the proper safety gear and equipment to knowing the weather and trail etiquette, a little advance preparation helps you enjoy your mountain biking experience to the fullest.

Equipment, Clothing, Helmet

You rely on your gear to keep you happy and safe in the woods, so always make sure your bike is in good working order. If you hear creaking, clunking, or other strange noises, get your bike tuned up. Learn to be self-sufficient on the trail. Know how to fix a flat tire or busted brake cable and how to administer basic first aid for yourself or another rider. At a minimum, carry the following items with you, along with The Mountaineers' Ten Essentials (see sidebar below):

- Extra tube
- Patch kit
- Tire pump
- Tire levers
- Chain tool and extra link
- Spoke wrench
- Multi-tool with various Allen wrench sizes
- First-aid kit

Having the appropriate clothing can make your mountain bike ride safer and more enjoyable. Since nasty weather can occur year round, I always carry an extra layer and a lightweight wind and rain jacket. Investing in high-quality bike shorts, synthetic or wool tops, and good socks and gloves will also improve comfort and allow you to spend more time on the bike. Eye protection is also a good idea to keep dust out of your eyes and protect yourself from those pokey manzanita bushes.

And a helmet? Wear one. Always.

Food and Hydration

Whether you are going for a 4-mile ride or a 40-mile ride, remember that your body needs fuel and liquids to perform at its best. Foods with a higher

The Ten Essentials: A Systems Approach
1. Navigation (map and compass)
2. Sun protection (sunglasses and sunscreen)
3. Insulation (extra clothing)
4. Illumination (headlamp or flashlight)
5. First-aid supplies
6. Fire (firestarter and matches/lighter)
7. Repair kit and tools (including knife)
8. Nutrition (extra food)
9. Hydration (extra water)
10. Emergency shelter

—The Mountaineers

carbohydrate-to-protein mix are usually preferred, but everyone is different; so bring along food that works for you so you don't "bonk" on a ride. There are so many options for bars, gels, gummies, and sports drinks, and most of them are small enough to fit in a pocket. Water is absolutely essential in central Oregon. Most rides are devoid of water on the route, so if you are planning on a longer outing, make sure you bring ample water.

Skills and Fitness
Those rides at the beginning of the season are usually the hardest—your legs feel like lead, you are sucking wind with every breath, and you keep thinking, "Why am I going so slow? Are my brakes dragging?" Mountain biking takes effort, and even naturally athletic and skilled riders spend hours on the bike becoming fitter and improving their skills. Seriously, training is effective and you'll have way more fun if you are physically fit. The same goes for skills—practice, practice, practice those skills so you can use them on the trails.

Weather and Climate
The weather in the high desert and Cascade mountains can vary greatly month to month, day to day, and even hour to hour. But most of the time around Bend the climate is conducive to riding. Bend's weather is generally dry with an average annual precipitation of just twelve inches a year, most of that arriving as snowfall in winter.

Springtime weather varies from calm sunshine to stormy thunder and hail. Every spring I find myself stuck in the Phil's Trail network in a driving hailstorm, only to ride home in warm sunshine. Summer's weather is more stable than spring's, but summer afternoon thunderstorms can bring violent downpours and the risk of lightning. Be prepared to handle a sudden deluge, and pay attention to where you are traveling if you think lightning is a risk. Summer daytime temperatures range from 50 to 100 degrees Fahrenheit—except in the nearby mountains, where nighttime temperatures can drop below freezing, even in the middle of summer. Bring warm layers! Early mornings are often the best time to ride in the summer. Fall is a great time for mountain biking here, with cool mornings and clear, sunny days.

In winter, Bend typically has a whole month (usually December or January) with snow on the ground, making mountain biking impossible. Even without snow cover, expect cold temperatures and, if the winter mountain biking trails are accessible, take care that you aren't damaging the trails by riding when they are wet and muddy during freeze-thaw cycles.

Traversing the top of Lookout Mountain, Routes 36 and 37

But sometimes a little moisture is a welcome thing in central Oregon—especially during the summer. After a good summer rainstorm or thunderstorm, the dry, dusty trails become fast and sticky, what we like to call "dirt perfect." So as long as it's not muddy, get out there!

CONSERVE, PROTECT, AND SHARE
Mountain biking is a form of backcountry travel. Simply being on the trails in the backcountry affects the immediate environment. It also means you are part of a community of outdoor enthusiasts. Always practice simple Leave No Trace principles to minimize your impact. One of the easiest ways to

Leave No Trace
- **Plan ahead and prepare.** Know where you are going and stay updated about any trail closures, regulations, or special concerns for the area you will visit. Be prepared in case of inclement weather, gear failure, hazards, or emergencies.
- **Travel and camp on durable surfaces.** For mountain biking, this means staying on the trail—not riding around obstacles—and keeping singletrack single.
- **Dispose of waste properly.** Pack it in, pack it out, and watch for the flyaway food wrappers.
- **Leave what you find.** Don't disturb the natural geology and ecology.
- **Minimize campfire impacts.** In the dry climate of central Oregon, fire is a big threat to the forests, wildlife, and nearby communities. Use a camp stove.
- **Respect wildlife.** Respect any temporary, seasonal, or permanent wildlife closures. Don't chase, follow, get close to, or otherwise disturb wildlife.
- **Be considerate of other visitors.** Look, listen, and smile—and yield appropriately to other trail users.

For more information on Leave No Trace principles, visit www.lnt.org.

protect the natural area around you is to avoid riding off the trail for any reason. We all love singletrack, so keep it "single" by staying on the trail.

Trail Etiquette and Being Nice

Depending on what you are used to, you might judge central Oregon mountain bike trails as relatively deserted or as completely overcrowded. It's all relative, right? One thing is for sure: Bend mountain bike trails are becoming more popular and beloved by locals and visitors alike, on and off bikes. It's important to know that you will see other users on the trails, and you will need to share the trails with them.

Many of the rides listed in this guidebook are mountain bike specific: they were built by mountain bikers and are primarily used and maintained by mountain bikers. All of the trails I've listed in this guide are closed to motorcycles and other motorized off-road vehicles. However, note that some of the rides include dirt roads and paved roads that may be used by cars, trucks, off-highway vehicles (OHVs), or motorcycles. Also be aware that hikers, dog walkers, runners, and horseback riders enjoy these trails and dirt roads as well, so yield appropriately. In the end, a little awareness, a lot of common courtesy, and a big smile will go a long way. And having a little lightweight bell on your bike is a great idea to let other trail users know that you are around the corner.

IMBA's Rules of the Trail
The International Mountain Bicycling Association (IMBA) is the largest group working directly to enhance and expand mountain biking opportunities around the world. IMBA developed their "Rules of the Trail" to promote

The Deschutes National Forest works to protect our forests from catastrophic fires, like the one that hit Cache Mountain, Route 41, in 2003. (Photo: Chris Kratsch)

responsible and courteous conduct on shared-use trails. Keep in mind that conventions for yielding and passing may vary in different locations, or with traffic conditions.

1. **Ride Open Trails:** Respect trail and road closures—ask a land manager for clarification if you are uncertain about the status of a trail. Do not trespass on private land. Obtain permits or other authorization as required. Be aware that bicycles are not permitted in areas protected as state or federal wilderness.

2. **Leave No Trace:** Be sensitive to the dirt beneath you. Wet and muddy trails are more vulnerable to damage than dry ones. When the trail is soft, consider other riding options. This also means staying on existing trails and not creating new ones. Don't cut switchbacks. Be sure to pack out at least as much as you pack in.

3. **Control Your Bicycle:** Inattention for even a moment could put yourself and others at risk. Obey all bicycle speed regulations and recommendations, and ride within your limits.

4. **Yield Appropriately:** Do your utmost to let your fellow trail users know you're coming—a friendly greeting or bell ring are good methods. Try to anticipate other trail users as you ride around corners. Bicyclists should yield to other nonmotorized trail users, unless the trail is clearly signed for bike-only travel. Bicyclists traveling downhill should yield to ones headed uphill, unless the trail is clearly signed for one-way or downhill-only traffic. In general, strive to make each pass a safe and courteous one.

5. **Never Scare Animals:** Animals are easily startled by an unannounced approach, a sudden movement, or a loud noise. Give animals enough room and time to adjust to you. When passing horses, use special care and follow directions from the horseback riders (ask if uncertain). Running cattle and disturbing wildlife are serious offenses.

6. **Plan Ahead:** Know your equipment, your ability, and the area in which you are riding and prepare accordingly. Strive to be self-sufficient: keep your equipment in good repair and carry necessary supplies for changes in weather or other conditions. Always wear a helmet and appropriate safety gear.

Electric Bikes and Fat Bikes

Mountain bike equipment is always changing, most recently with the rise of fat bikes and electric bikes.

COTA's Trail Love

The Central Oregon Trail Alliance (COTA), in an effort to bring a local flavor to trail etiquette, developed its "Trail Love" campaign to keep everyone happy on the trails.

Share the Trail Love with these simple guidelines.

1. **Look, Listen, Smile:** As trail users, we rely on one another. Have fun, and keep your eyes and ears open. Smile and say hello! You are in one of the best mountain bike areas in the nation.

2. **Descending Riders Stop for Others:** We all love the downhill, but skidding out of control is not cool. Expect some uphill riders and be ready to move to one side of the trail, stopping until your line is clear.

3. **Tread on Trail:** Thanks for yielding to other riders—but remember that riding off into the bushes widens and damages trails. Instead, put a foot down and feel good knowing that tread on the trail keeps singletrack narrow and fun.

Fat bikes have extra-large, balloon-like tires that can roll easily over many obstacles. They originated specifically for use on sand or snow, but many mountain bikers prefer to ride them on singletrack as well. Remember, just because a fat bike can handle more challenging terrain, the rules of the trail still apply—stay on the trail and keep singletrack single.

Electric bikes, or e-bikes, are electric-motor-assisted mountain bikes. While currently gaining popularity in Europe, e-bikes haven't yet taken off here in the States, but many people think they will become more popular

Riding in the mud can cause lasting trail damage.

over time. Here's the simple land manager policy on e-bikes: they are considered to be motorized bikes and are not allowed on nonmotorized trails. Note, too, that wheeled vehicles of any kind, including all bikes (and excepting wheelchairs), are not allowed in federally designated wilderness areas without a special permit (e.g., for wheelchairs). This applies to the wilderness sections of the Waldo Lake area and the Three Sisters Wilderness.

KNOW WHEN TO GO

Lucky for us, many of the trails listed in this guidebook are open to mountain bikes when they are clear of snow and downed trees, but there are a few exceptions and a few precautions that you might consider at certain times.

Wildlife closures: Some trails have seasonal wildlife closures (see Route 1, The Maston; Route 5, Otter Bench; and Routes 14 and 19, which include Flagline Trail), so pay attention and ask the land manager or one of the trail organizations about seasonal rules if you are not sure.

Forest thinning and prescribed burning: Humans have managed the central Oregon forests to restrict natural fire for well over the last century, resulting today in unnatural forest conditions—overly dense forests with a thick understory. These conditions create an alarmingly high fire risk that threatens nearby communities. Recently, the Deschutes National Forest has started to take a proactive approach to restoring the forests to their original state—large, old trees with an open understory.

Through the year 2020, there will be temporary forest and trail closures to accommodate the work of restoring our forests back to health. Visit the Deschutes Collaborative Forest's website for updated information on closures: www.deschutescollaborativeforest.org.

Hunting season: More than once while on my favorite biking trails, I've come across hunters in full camouflage, startling me into remembering it was hunting season. (They are hard to see: that camo stuff really works!) In the busiest areas, like those west of Bend and in the Wanoga complex, where mountain bikers way outnumber hunters, this isn't as much of an issue. But once you get into the High Cascades, around Waldo Lake, or especially up in the Ochoco Mountains, expect that you might see hunters. Generally speaking, bow season is usually all of September, and rifle deer season starts the first weekend in October and lasts through the end of the month. Stay alert, wear bright colors to make sure you can be seen, and remember to share the trail.

Freeze-thaw on trails: Central Oregon doesn't have a distinct "mud season" like other parts of the country, when the snow melts all at once leaving a persistent layer of gooey, messy mud on most trails. We can, however, have a ferocious "freeze-thaw" cycle in late winter and early spring that can impact your riding experience and the trails. Ground moisture freezes at night, to be released again during the day when the temperatures climb above freezing. If your tire rolls through that muddy mess, it will leave a track, which forms a channel that traps the water instead of letting it dry. Eventually, the center of the trail erodes out, creating even worse conditions, enticing riders to ride around the mud, which makes the trails wider. Keep singletrack single; stay off the trails during a freeze-thaw cycle.

To avoid the freeze-thaw cycle, another option is to ride winter trails when the ground is completely frozen and there is absolutely no chance of it thawing out while you are riding. This means you ride in subfreezing temperatures, which is only for the toughest of mountain bikers. If you choose to ride on trails that have frozen spots of ice or snow, be careful. An innocuous corner in summer conditions can send you sideways if there is a patch of ice on it in winter.

Races and events: Bend is becoming a popular place for mountain biking and trail running races. Although the trails don't officially close for such events, it's not very fun to ride in the middle of a race, unless you're one of the racers, of course. Check with a local shop about scheduled events and races.

HOW TO USE
THIS GUIDE

Listed in this guidebook are forty-six routes, ranging from the shortest trail network of less than 3 miles to epic rides of up to 30 miles. A route may be composed of a single trail or several connecting trails.

This guidebook is intended, first, to give mountain bikers accurate routes and descriptions and, second, to offer up the best way to enjoy the trails in central Oregon. I've done my best not only to include every trail but to piece together rides that are popular and fun. I've sought the best climbs and the best downhills, and routes that offer good scenery or solitude. These are not just my preferences but the result of talking with some of the most dedicated mountain bikers in Bend. Of course, these selections are all subjective. I'm sure there have been many heated debates at the local pubs about the proper way to ride certain trails. You are free to follow your own path, but I hope these rides as I've laid them out are as much fun for you as they are for me.

Note, too, that some of the rides I have chosen, particularly those west of Bend and in the Wanoga complex, are linked. That means that you can either ride the described route, or you can add on other trails to make a longer ride. I recommend referencing the most accurate and commonly used hard-copy maps, called Adventure Maps, to get a full understanding of the interconnected trail systems and extensive route options in central Oregon.

The routes in this book are divided along natural, generally geographic lines into eight regional sections. "North of Bend" includes popular winter and spring rides near Tumalo, Redmond, and Terrebonne. "West of Bend and

Opposite: *Lava rock outcroppings are common on central Oregon trails.*

Wanoga" describes the best-known, most popular rides that are closest to Bend. "High Cascades" includes midsummer to late-summer rides situated at the crest of the Cascades and near high mountain lakes. "Waldo Lake" features routes on the west side of the Cascade crest—the farthest rides from Bend described in this guide, though all very popular and often accessed from Bend.

"East and South of Bend" includes high-desert-style rides in juniper and sagebrush, marked by ancient lava volcanoes. "Crook County and Ochoco Mountains" is centered on rides around the town of Prineville, about a one-hour drive northeast of Bend, which showcases very different terrain and ecology than the Cascades. The "Sisters" routes are near the quaint tourist town of Sisters. And lastly the "McKenzie River" section features trails located on the west side of the Oregon Cascades that are also quite accessible from Bend; it's a two-hour drive from high desert to the green McKenzie River valley.

RIDE TYPE

Rides are categorized as loop, out-and-back, shuttle, or network.

Loop. A loop starts and ends at the same place, but with new scenery throughout—unlike an out-and-back ride. Note that some loops look like a "lollipop," which is an out-and-back section combined with a loop.

Out-and-back. Most out-and-backs are on a single trail, but some include more than one trail. Some out-and-back rides are also of the "lollipop" variety, meaning they are out-and-back with a shorter loop attached (for example, Route 43, Suttle Tie to Suttle Lake). Ride descriptions and mileages include the entire ride from end to end and back again, but you can turn around whenever you want.

Shuttle. A handful of the rides are popular one-way shuttles, where you start at one point and end at another point. You can arrange your own car shuttle or use a shuttle service (see Resources, Guides and Shuttle Services).

Network. A few rides are designated as "network," which includes an outer loop with many other trails inside the loop that can be connected together as you wish. In these cases, either I have described the "main loop" in detail or I have tried to describe the general lay of the land and the nature of the trails.

TRAIL TYPE

This section breaks the route down into singletrack, dirt road, and/or pavement, providing a rough percentage of each surface you'll find on the ride. What I've designated as "dirt roads" can be dirt or gravel and may have a varying amount of usage, from wide, heavily used gravel roads to narrow, seldom used "doubletrack." Many of the dirt roads are also open to motorized use, such as cars, trucks, OHVs, and motorcycles. Always remember that you share the roads with other users.

DISTANCE

Ride distances, rounded to the nearest tenth of a mile, were calculated using GPS. GPS and mapping technologies can vary, and when I cross-checked to Strava or Garmin Connect I sometimes found discrepancies in tracked distances. In cases where my mapped distances differed from those listed on the Adventure Maps or from other riders' published distances, I went with the distances that most closely matched those on the Adventure Maps.

ELEVATION GAIN/LOSS

The elevations listed for the rides are total elevation gain and loss in feet, rounded to the nearest ten feet. As such, loop and out-and-back rides will have the same number for elevation gain and loss, and one-way shuttles will have different figures for gain and loss. I found that when I cross-checked to Strava or Garmin Connect, some rides also had differing elevation values. Elevation numbers were gathered directly from my GPX files (the mapping files that came direct from the GPS device), which were then imported into CalTopo, the online mapping tool that I used to create the individual ride maps in this guide.

HIGH POINT

High points for each ride are listed in feet above sea level.

RIDE TIME

Ride time is the average time it takes for most riders to complete the route. Some people like to cruise and spend a lot of time stopping to check out the scenery. Others like to hammer, no matter what. Ride times also vary depending on rider fitness, skill, and energy level for that day. Keep in mind, too, that weather, trail conditions, and mechanical mishaps can rapidly change the length of a ride.

DIFFICULTY RATINGS

Ride ratings are broken down into technical difficulty and fitness intensity, ratings that sometimes match, but not always. Of course, the challenge

There are miles and miles of singletrack in the Wanoga area, Routes 11-13.

of a trail or route is subjective—what may be easy for some might be nearly impossible for others. Some riders have a technical riding prowess that rivals that of a pro mountain biker, but they may not be fit enough to ride more than 15 miles. Other riders can climb relentlessly, yet they have mediocre technical skills. Use these ratings as a guide to help you make informed decisions and choose rides that best suit your abilities, energy, and fitness level.

Generally speaking, the trails around the Bend region are considered to be gentler and less technical than those in many other mountain biking regions in the United States. We simply don't have the steep landscape of Oakridge, Oregon, or the tons of rock around Moab, Utah. The beauty of our trails is twofold: they are easy to access and they are accessible to all levels of riders. Generally, the higher you go in elevation, the harder they get.

I've added the word "epic" to some ride descriptions, usually because the trails rank both solidly "expert" in technical difficulty and "very strenuous" in fitness intensity.

Routefinding is a factor that adds difficulty to a ride. Some rides have good signage and are obvious and easy to navigate; others have few to no signs and patch together what seem like random sections of trail and/or roads, which makes routefinding challenging. Most of these rides require moderate routefinding skills, since many intersections are not signed and parts of the ride can seem confusing. Carry a compass; knowing how to use one is a helpful skill in any outdoor activity.

Technical Difficulty

A ride's technical difficulty—beginner, intermediate, advanced, or expert—is based on ability to negotiate the tread without getting off your bike.

- **Beginner:** Easy trails that are generally flat, smooth, and stable, often with a wider trail tread and few obstacles or steep sections.
- **Intermediate:** Trail tread is narrower and includes the occasional smaller, generally rollable, but unavoidable obstacle, such as rocks or roots, and has steeper sections of trail.
- **Advanced:** Trail tread is narrow or often uneven with slightly steeper grades and unavoidable obstacles in the trail like rocks, roots, or loose soil that require more advanced skills to negotiate safely.
- **Expert:** The most difficult trails with nearly continuous uneven tread from rocks, roots, and loose dirt. These trails feature steeper grades and larger unavoidable obstacles including rollovers, small to large drops, possible exposure above small cliffs or steep slopes, and long, challenging rock gardens.

In most cases, the technical challenges of a trail will be limited to short sections, easily walked. In the advanced- and expert-level rides, there may also be some obstacles that are too difficult to ride, either up or down. These sections are considered "hike-a-bike" and are walked by most, if not all, riders.

Note that a small percentage of riders believe in the "no dab" theory (no feet on the ground) and, rather than walk, will ride around obstacles in the trail, such as rocks or logs, thereby widening the trail or even creating new renegade trails. This is not the best situation when we're trying to keep singletrack "single." Bottom line—there is no shame in walking.

Fitness Intensity

The scale of effort or fitness intensity for rides ranges from easy to very strenuous and is quantified by both total mileage ridden and vertical feet of climbing.

- **Easy:** 10 miles or less and/or 1000 feet of vertical gain.
- **Moderate:** 10–15 miles and/or between 1000 and 2000 feet of vertical gain.
- **Strenuous:** 15–25 miles and/or between 2000 and 3000 feet of vertical gain.
- **Very strenuous:** 25+ miles and/or over 3000 feet of vertical gain.

Rides with mixed intensity will always be rated the more difficult of the two ratings. For example, if a ride is only 12 miles but has 2700 feet of vertical gain, it will be rated as strenuous, not moderate. Hopefully these ratings will be helpful in matching your fitness and energy level to the appropriate ride.

SEASON

Season represents the months, on average, that the routes are rollable and free of snow and reflects preferred times, when they are most enjoyable. Over the last twenty years of riding in central Oregon and the Cascades, I've seen noticeable seasonal changes. Seasonal snowpack seems to shrink each year and the trails are clear of snow earlier, creating longer "summer" seasons. Note that the conditions can change rapidly during certain times of the year, For instance, the trails may be rideable if we have a dry February but then close down in March thanks to a big springtime snowstorm that dumps a few inches of snow on the ground.

Also, mountain weather can be unpredictable at best. It is not uncommon to get snow in the high country during any month, even in July or August. While all "winter" rides can be ridden year round (unless they are covered in snow), in the heat of summer they can be quite dry and sandy, making them less enjoyable for biking.

A NOTE ABOUT SAFETY

Safety is an important concern in all outdoor activities. No guide-book can alert you to every hazard or anticipate the limitations of every reader. The descriptions of roads, trails, routes, and natural features in this book are not representations that a particular place or excursion will be safe for your party or appropriate for their level of skill and experience. As such, all users of this guide assume any and all risks associated with riding a mountain bike on the routes and terrain described herein. Safety is solely your responsibility: under normal conditions, mountain bike excursions require the usual attention to traffic, road and trail conditions, weather, terrain, the capabilities of your party, and other factors. Always wear a properly fitting helmet and be prepared to deal with changing weather, mechanical issues, and first-aid needs on the trail. Keep informed on current conditions and exercise common sense for a safe, enjoyable outing. The publisher and author are not responsible for any adverse consequences resulting directly or indirectly from information contained in this book.

—Mountaineers Books

MAP

Supplementary maps are often incredibly helpful, especially if you want to link several routes or trails together. Here, I've listed the best alternative map option for each route. Almost all the rides are included on the following maps in the Adventure Maps series: *Bend, Oregon Trail Map*; *Sisters & Redmond High Desert Trail Map*; and *Oakridge, Oregon Trail Map*. The Adventure Maps are accurate and waterproof and can be found in nearly every bike shop in Bend. For a fee you can also download them online from www .adventuremaps.net.

GPS

These are the GPS coordinates for the start of each ride, listed in the decimal degrees format (for example: 44.2114° N, -121.3032° W), using the WGS84 datum. For shuttle rides, coordinates are listed for both the start and the end of the described ride.

LAND MANAGER

In central Oregon, nearly all of our rides are on public lands, managed by government agencies such as the US Forest Service, Bureau of Land Management, and Oregon Parks and Recreation Department. I've listed the relevant land managers for each ride.

PERMIT

Unless noted in the information block for a specific ride—and there are a few—a permit is not needed to ride on any of the trails described. Trailhead fees for parking, if required, are listed in the ride overview.

OVERVIEW

This section gives you the overall essence of the ride, including terrain, steepness, ecology, geology, points of interest, and views.

GETTING THERE

Each route includes driving directions to the ride start and, for one-way shuttles, how to get to the shuttle end. For rides within roughly 20 miles of Bend, the description starts in the center of Bend, at the intersection of NE 3rd Street and NE Greenwood Avenue. For the routes listed that are more than 20 miles from Bend, the description will usually say something similar to: "From Bend, take US Highway 20 West to the town of Sisters." Note that parking space is limited at some trailheads, particularly Phil's trailhead. If you live in Bend or are staying there, consider riding your bike to the trailhead. It gives you a nice warm-up and is one less car on the roads and in the parking lot.

As a reference for driving directions, Google Maps has the most accurate and updated maps.

MILEAGE LOG

The mileage listed for each ride matches the mile-by-mile description of the recommended route. On out-and-back rides, I have described the total mileage for the complete ride to the end of the trail and back. On those rides, of course, you can easily shorten the ride by turning around whenever you like.

OPTIONS

Many of the trails described here are interconnected, so I've often recommended route options: specific options within the mileage logs and more general options just following the mileage logs. Know that these ride options may make the suggested route longer or shorter or leave you in an entirely different place than that described in the overview.

ROUTE MAP

Each route features an accompanying map. Where a ride starts and finishes in the same place, only the trailhead symbol is used. When parking is at the trailhead, it is not labeled separately.

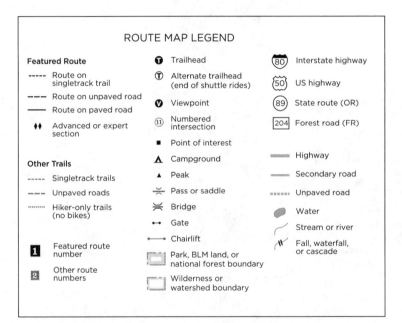

ROUTE MAP LEGEND

Featured Route

- - - - Route on singletrack trail

— — — Route on unpaved road

——— Route on paved road

♦♦ Advanced or expert section

Other Trails

- - - - Singletrack trails

— — — Unpaved roads

········· Hiker-only trails (no bikes)

1 Featured route number

2 Other route numbers

🅣 Trailhead

🅣 Alternate trailhead (end of shuttle rides)

🅥 Viewpoint

⑪ Numbered intersection

■ Point of interest

▲ Campground

▲ Peak

⤨ Pass or saddle

⤨ Bridge

•–• Gate

•——• Chairlift

Park, BLM land, or national forest boundary

Wilderness or watershed boundary

(80) Interstate highway

(50) US highway

(89) State route (OR)

204 Forest road (FR)

═══ Highway

═══ Secondary road

═════ Unpaved road

Water

Stream or river

Fall, waterfall, or cascade

NORTH OF BEND

The communities north of Bend, including Tumalo, Redmond, and Terrebonne, typically get less snow and are a bit warmer than everything to the south. This makes for nice options for winter riding. Since the early 2000s, these areas (most of which are on public lands managed by either the Bureau of Land Management or US Forest Service) have seen a rebirth in popularity, with the Central Oregon Trail Alliance (COTA) working diligently to design and build trails tailored to mountain bikes.

The five rides listed in this section each have their own character, but most include wide-open vistas, sage-covered hillsides, old-growth juniper, and a variety of tread. The Maston (Route 1) is smooth, flat, and fast, and is great for beginners; the rides in Smith Rock State Park and the Crooked River National Grassland (Routes 3–5) are rockier and more technical for more advanced riders. In the next few years, the BLM plans to develop more trails on Cline Butte, which is just across the road from The Maston. This will expand that network into a full day's riding in that area.

A word of caution: Although the trails north of Bend are prime for winter riding, there are times when the trails are too muddy. Don't even attempt to ride Gray Butte Trail in the Grasslands (Route 4) if you think it will be muddy. Thanks to high levels of clay, it turns into a peanut butter–like substance that becomes impossible to ride through and will leave you cleaning your bike for hours afterward. Also watch for the pesky freeze-thaw cycle at The Maston, as this is when conditions can be most challenging. Check with local bike shops Trinity Bikes or Hutch's of Redmond for current trail conditions.

Opposite: *Trails to the north of Bend wind through open, high-desert landscapes.*

Most of these trails are nonmotorized multiuser trails, so expect to see hikers, horseback riders, runners, dog walkers, and, in Smith Rock State Park, rock climbers. Camping options are scarce near many of the ride areas, with two exceptions: there is great camping at Skull Hollow Campground in the Grasslands and at the Smith Rock State Park Bivouac Area (The Bivy). Fortunately there are plenty of options for hotels. For post-ride grub you also have a wealth of choices. In Redmond I prefer a big plate of tacos at La Fondita, or pub fare at the Pig and Pound Public House. Just outside of Terrebonne, the Terrebonne Depot is a converted train station that is a favorite of Smith Rock climbers. They have a full menu of good eats and a sunny deck to enjoy a post-ride brew.

1 THE MASTON

LOOP

Trail Type: 100% singletrack
Distance: 11.6 miles
Elevation Gain/Loss: 520/520 feet
High Point: 3236 feet
Ride Time: 1–3 hours
Technical Difficulty: Beginner–intermediate
Fitness Intensity: Easy

Season: Year-round, best in winter and spring
Map: Adventure Maps, Sisters & Redmond High Desert Trail Map
GPS: 44.2114° N, -121.3032° W
Land Manager: Bureau of Land Management, Prineville District

OVERVIEW

The Maston is a complex of 19 miles of trails on a relatively flat plateau above the Deschutes River canyon between Bend and Redmond. There are several loops and route options, all of which wind through old-growth junipers and sagebrush. Make sure to take a map with you to explore this trail network. These trails were built in the mid-2000s as a winter riding area for when most other trails are covered in snow. The Maston is an excellent example of mountain bikers and equestrians peacefully sharing the same trail area. COTA and the BLM worked together to provide "separate but equal" trails for all users. This is also a popular area for trail runners due to its flat nature and mild climate.

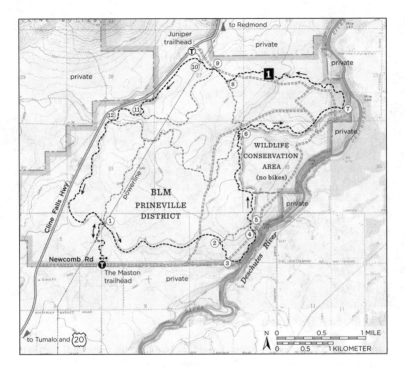

Most of The Maston's trails wind through relatively flat, smooth terrain, with the exception of a short section that skirts the river canyon, offering scenic views and a wee bit of exposure. The river canyon is host to golden and bald eagles; and while that portion of trail is always open, the remaining land along the canyon is closed for eagle nesting. Please adhere to any signs.

While this is a popular winter riding area, do not ride here in any degree of wet conditions, as this area can be very muddy during intermittent winter snow-thaw cycles. And if you do find yourself in the mud, please ride right through the middle of it. Riding around muddy spots widens the trail and harms the singletrack. Before you go, inquire at one of the Redmond bike shops about current conditions.

I've listed this ride with a technical difficulty of beginner to intermediate. For the most part, the trails are smooth and fast with few rocks. However,

A winter day at The Maston

there are some sections of rocky tread that require a bit more skill, particularly near the river canyon and on the eastern side of the trail network.

The ride I've described here is a suggested counterclockwise route that takes the outermost trails of the network. See the map for alternative options. Trail intersections are all signed and numbered, and these numbers are noted on the map and in the mileage log.

GETTING THERE

From Bend, take US Highway 20 West toward Sisters. After crossing the Deschutes River, turn right in Tumalo on Cline Falls Highway (Cook Avenue). Drive north for 4.7 miles to Newcomb Road and turn right. This is a dusty gravel road, so check your speed so you don't dust the nearby houses. The parking lot and trailhead will be in 0.8 mile on the left side of Newcomb Road. An additional small trailhead, the Juniper trailhead, can be found 3 miles farther north on Cline Falls Highway.

MILEAGE LOG

0.0 From The Maston trailhead, take the main mountain biking trail through the gate to the north.

0.3 Turn right at the first intersection (1), right below the powerline. This section of trail follows a historic canal.

2.0 Turn right at signed intersection (2).

2.4 Turn left at signed intersection (3). From here, you will enter a more technical section of trail high above the river canyon, with some exposed sections. Stay straight through intersection (4).

3.4 Stay on the singletrack (ignoring the dirt road you cross over) to turn right at intersection (5) for a brief descent.

4.6 Turn right at intersection (6) and descend to the lowest elevation section of trail.

6.1 Turn left at intersection (7). From here, you often have nice views of Smith Rock in the distance.

7.5 Turn right at intersection (8).

7.7 Turn right at intersection (9).

8.0 Turn left at intersection (10). If you were to go straight/right, you would reach the Juniper trailhead. Enjoy beautiful views of the Three Sisters mountains.

9.1 Turn right at intersection (11).

9.6 Turn right at intersection (12). Follow this trail back to intersection (1).

11.3 At intersection (1), turn right, back toward The Maston trailhead.

11.6 Return to the trailhead where you started.

2 RADLANDS

NETWORK

Trail Type: 100% singletrack
Distance: Up to 9 miles
Elevation Gain/Loss: 360/360 feet
High Point: 3053 feet
Ride Time: 1–2 hours
Technical Difficulty: Advanced
Fitness Intensity: Easy

Season: Year-round, best in winter and spring
Map: Adventure Maps, Sisters & Redmond High Desert Trail Map
GPS: 44.2919° N, -121.1461° W
Land Manager: Redmond Area Park and Recreation District

Riding through juniper and sage country at Radlands

OVERVIEW

Radlands is a unique trail system on public property owned by Deschutes County and managed by the Redmond Area Park and Recreation District (RAPRD). This is a very small network of trails, but due to its location and weather, it is often the only viable mountain biking option in the heart of winter when snow covers all other trails.

The trails here are fairly rocky, with lava rock outcroppings and small ramps to ride up and down. It is a great choice for anyone looking for a quick ride to challenge their technical skills. The area has some old-growth juniper trees and good views of Smith Rock State Park to the north. Don't be alarmed if you hear a strange buzzing noise or gunshots. Radlands is next to a radio airplane field and a shooting range.

Unfortunately, because this trail network is adjacent to town, it also suffers from copious amounts of garbage and the occasional homeless encampment. RAPRD and COTA are working to improve the area by keeping it clean and building new sections of trail. They are always looking for volunteers to help out.

GETTING THERE

From Bend, take US Highway 97 North 15 miles to Redmond. In Redmond, turn right onto NE Negus Way and drive east. In 0.7 mile, the main road

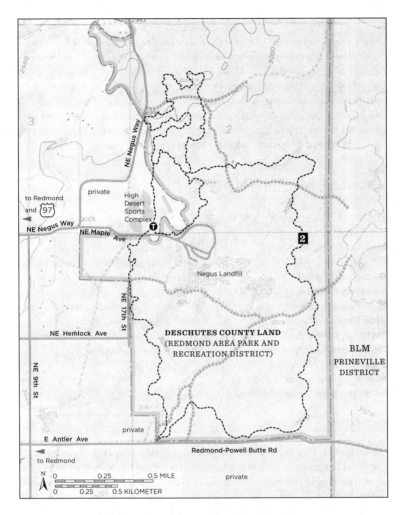

turns sharply to the left. Go straight here onto NE Maple Avenue. In another 0.3 mile, turn left into the High Desert Sports Complex and park here at the trailhead.

MILEAGE LOG

This is one of a handful of trail networks that doesn't warrant a suggested route. There are two main areas in Radlands: short loops north of the trailhead and NE Maple Avenue, and a longer loop to the south. Because these trails have very little elevation gain or loss, they are great to explore riding in either direction. The total mileage for singletrack is about 9 miles, so you can actually get in an 18-mile ride if you ride the loops one way, then turn around and ride them again in the other direction. Take the map with you and explore one of central Oregon's newest trail systems.

3 SMITH ROCK

LOOP

Trail Type: 85% singletrack, 15% dirt road
Distance: 12.1 miles
Elevation Gain/Loss: 2360/2360 feet
High Point: 3809 feet
Ride Time: 2–4 hours
Technical Difficulty: Advanced
Fitness Intensity: Strenuous
Season: March–November
Map: Adventure Maps, Sisters & Redmond High Desert Trail Map

GPS: 44.3668° N, -121.1362° W
Land Managers: Oregon Parks and Recreation Department; Bureau of Land Management, Prineville District; Ochoco National Forest and Crooked River National Grassland
Permit: Oregon State Parks annual or day-use parking permit

OVERVIEW

Smith Rock is a geologic wonderland, and this ride affords the best views of this world-renowned rock climbing area, including the Monkey Face spire, as well as views of snowy Cascade peaks in the distance. The route described below includes a loop through the park, with an additional out-and-back through BLM lands and the Crooked River National Grassland on the Gray Butte Trail. It also takes you on Burma Road, one of the steepest, toughest dirt road climbs in central Oregon. When you are at the parking lot, you can see Burma Road to the east, so you can get an idea of what you are signing up for. Prepare for a grind!

A rider descends a rocky section of trail toward the Monkey Face spire at Smith Rock State Park. (Photo: Chris Kratsch)

You will likely encounter hikers, runners, and climbers, especially on a sunny spring weekend. Take care around blind corners, yield as needed, and be courteous to other users. This is an Oregon State Park, so you are required to purchase a day-use parking pass. At the time of writing, the fee is $5/day.

GETTING THERE

From Bend, take US Highway 97 North about 20 miles to the community of Terrebonne. In Terrebonne, turn right on B Avenue (NE Smith Rock Way). In 1.6 miles, turn left on NE 17th Street. In 0.5 mile, turn right on NE Wilcox Avenue. Take the next left, in 0.6 mile, on NE Crooked River Drive. Park at the main Smith Rock day-use area.

MILEAGE LOG

0.0 From the Smith Rock day-use parking area, take the dirt road toward Smith Rock (there is a very short section of pavement at the top), descending down to the Crooked River and the main bridge.

0.5 At the four-way intersection, just past the bridge, turn right on Wolf Tree Trail.

1.3 The trail becomes very steep and you will likely start walking your bike up to the intersection with Burma Rd.

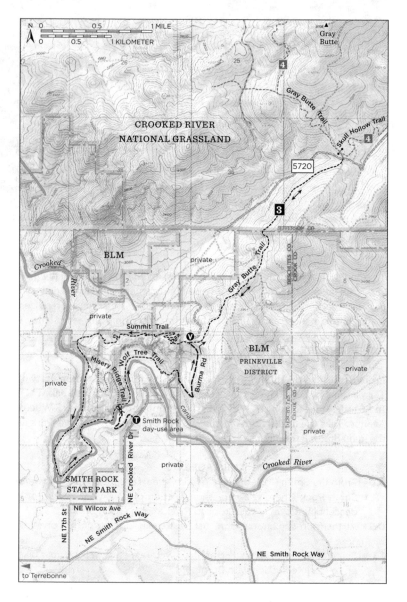

N
0   0.5   1 MILE
0   0.5   1 KILOMETER

Gray
Butte

CROOKED RIVER
NATIONAL GRASSLAND

Gray Butte Trail

Skull Hollow Trail

4

5720

3

JEFFERSON CO

Crooked
River

BLM

private

DESCHUTES CO
CROOK CO

private

Gray Butte Trail

Summit Trail

V

BLM
PRINEVILLE
DISTRICT

private

Misery Ridge Trail

Wolf Tree Trail

Burma Rd

private

canal

T Smith Rock
day-use area

NE Crooked River Dr

Smith Rock
day-use area

Crooked River

SMITH ROCK
STATE PARK

private

NE 17th St

NE Wilcox Ave

NE Smith Rock Way

NE Smith Rock Way

to Terrebonne

1.7 Get on Burma Rd. and prepare for a leg burner. Burma is steep and can also have loose tread. Put your head down and just get to the top.

2.4 At the top of Burma Rd., take a breather, then turn right onto Gray Butte Trail. The trail climbs at first, then contours over toward Gray Butte. You will pass through a few cattle gates. Please be sure to close the gates behind you.

4.8 This is the first Gray Butte saddle. For this out-and-back ride, turn around here and return to Burma Rd. *Option: You can stay left and continue farther on the Gray Butte Trail. It is 3.7 miles, much of it downhill, to the end of the trail at McCoin Orchard. You can choose to turn around at any point. The trail to the right will descend toward Skull Hollow. Don't go this way unless you are prepared to climb back up. (See Route 4, Grasslands, for details on both options.)*

7.2 You are now back at Burma Rd. Turn right onto the Summit Trail to follow a series of switchbacks that take you down to the backside of Smith Rock. Take in some awesome views here along the way.

9.2 The trail reaches the Crooked River again and you will wind around back to the main bridge. Watch for hikers and climbers along this section and follow the rules to yield as appropriate.

11.6 You are back at the main bridge that crosses the Crooked River. Go right, over the bridge, and take the unpaved road back up to the parking area.

12.1 Return to the main parking lot at the Smith Rock day-use area.

4 GRASSLANDS

LOOP

Trail Type: 80% singletrack, 20% dirt road
Distance: 9.3 miles
Elevation Gain/Loss: 1550/1550 feet
High Point: 4263 feet
Ride Time: 1–3 hours
Technical Difficulty: Advanced
Fitness Intensity: Moderate

Season: March–November
Map: Adventure Maps, Sisters & Redmond High Desert Trail Map
GPS: 44.3980° N, -121.0642° W
Land Manager: Ochoco National Forest and Crooked River National Grassland

OVERVIEW

Many people don't realize that just adjacent to Smith Rock State Park is the Crooked River National Grassland, which is managed by the Ochoco National Forest. In the early spring, this is one of the first areas to sprout little bits of greenery and tiny, bright wildflowers. Combined with awesome views and sunny weather, this loop is a great way to brush the cobwebs off in the springtime.

The ride follows the Skull Hollow Trail partway up, then takes a dirt road to the historic McCoin Orchard. The orchard dates back to 1886 when homesteaders claimed the land under the Homestead Act. Near the orchard, you'll get on the Gray Butte Trail. *Do not* attempt to ride this trail if there is any moisture in the ground or during a freeze-thaw cycle. The soil on Gray Butte is heavy clay that turns into an absolute mess when wet. Just turn around if you find yourself in those conditions and don't fall into the "it will get better" trap. It never does.

Watch for equestrians out here, especially on the final descent to Skull Hollow, which is ripping fast with blind corners. Make yourself heard. Also note that you will go through a few gates on this ride. Be sure to close them behind you.

GETTING THERE

From Bend, take US Highway 97 North about 20 miles to the community of Terrebonne. In Terrebonne, turn right on B Avenue (NE Smith Rock Way) and head east. In 4.8 miles, turn left onto Lone Pine Road. Follow Lone Pine Road for another 4.2 miles until you reach Forest Road 5710 at the entrance to the Skull Hollow Campground and trailhead. Turn left here and park in one of the large dirt parking lots.

MILEAGE LOG

0.0 From Skull Hollow trailhead, start on the Skull Hollow Trail. It is flat as it rolls through the campground, then climbs.

1.0 Find a short downhill trail to your right (there are a few options along this section of trail) that will take you down to FR 5710. Make sure you get to the road before it splits into FR 5710 and FR 5720; take the right fork to stay on FR 5710.

2.4 Turn left onto FR 57.

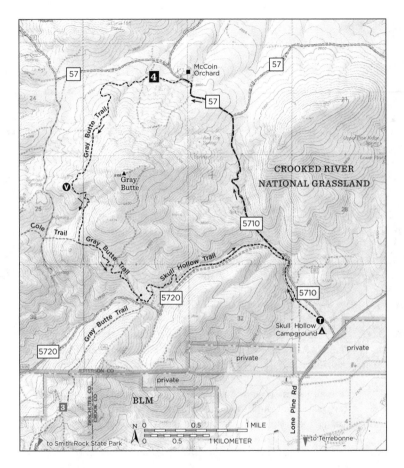

3.1 Look for the Gray Butte trailhead on your left, directly across the road from McCoin Orchard. Get on the Gray Butte Trail here. It will climb significantly for the next 1 to 2 miles. You'll pass through a cattle gate. Be sure to close it behind you.

4.9 Check out the rock outcropping and the fantastic viewpoint, then get back on the trail when you are ready.

5.1 You'll start descending with a few flat and rolly sections along the way.

The Gray Butte Trail is a long hillside traverse on narrow singletrack.
(Photo: Chris Kratsch)

5.7 At the intersection with the Cole Trail, stay left on Gray Butte Trail.

6.8 After passing through a gate, turn left on the Skull Hollow Trail to descend Skull Hollow. This section is super fast and fun. It can be damp down in the draw, so watch for slick spots.

8.0 Cross FR 5720, and continue down the Skull Hollow Trail back to your car.

9.3 Return to the Skull Hollow trailhead.

OPTIONS

The Cole Trail is another loop that you can add on to this ride that will nearly double the mileage. Take a map with you, and explore that trail and the connecting dirt roads if you wish.

5 OTTER BENCH

OUT-AND-BACK

Trail Type: 100% singletrack
Distance: 6.8 miles
Elevation Gain/Loss: 900/900 feet
High Point: 2544 feet
Ride Time: 1–2 hours
Technical Difficulty: Advanced
Fitness Intensity: Moderate
Season: Year-round, best October–April

Map: Adventure Maps, Sisters & Redmond High Desert Trail Map
GPS: 44.4623° N, -121.2826° W
Land Managers: Bureau of Land Management, Prineville District; Ochoco National Forest and Crooked River National Grassland

OVERVIEW

The Otter Bench trails are an interesting little group of trails with some spectacular scenery of the Crooked River Gorge. These trails are located on BLM land and the Crooked River National Grassland, at the very end of the lower neighborhoods of Crooked River Ranch, a rural community just northwest of Terrebonne. If you are willing to make the drive, then this is a fun and challenging ride.

There are only about 7 miles of trails, but you get your money's worth as almost half of the route is fairly challenging, with a lot of lava rock and a few sections of cliffside

View of Lake Billy Chinook and the Crooked River Gorge from Otter Bench

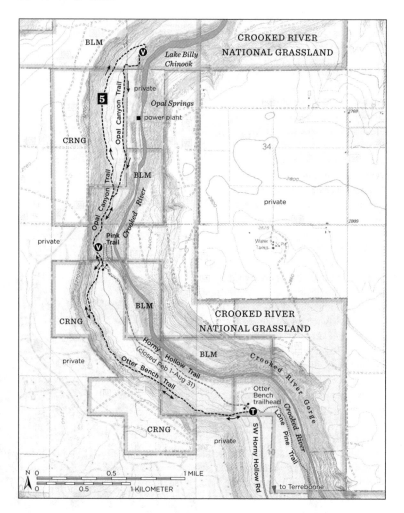

exposure. This is also rattlesnake country so be careful, especially in the spring and fall when they are sunning themselves on rocks to stay warm. You don't want to get bit or run one over. In the spring, there are nice wildflowers that try to distract you from the sublime views of the Crooked River far below you. The farthest end of the ride overlooks Lake Billy Chinook. This ride is best done in the early spring, late fall, or winter, when temperatures are mild. It can get quite hot up here in the summer, with no shade.

The route below excludes the Horny Hollow Trail because it is closed from February 1 to August 31 each year for wildlife, but from September 1 to January 31, you are welcome to ride it.

GETTING THERE

From Bend, take US Highway 97 North to Terrebonne. In Terrebonne, turn left on Lower Bridge Road and drive west. After 2 miles, turn right on 43rd Street. In another 1.7 miles, turn left onto Chinook Drive. In 5 miles, stay straight on SW Horny Hollow Road. Do not take Chinook Drive back up the hill. In another 1.7 miles, you will reach the end of the road and a small gravel parking lot. This is the Otter Bench trailhead. Park here.

MILEAGE LOG

0.0 From the trailhead, take the Otter Bench Trail to the left. If the Horny Hollow Trail is open, you can take that trail if desired.

1.7 At the intersection of the Otter Bench Trail with the Horny Hollow Trail (closed to bikes February 1–August 31) and the Pink Trail (closed to bikes year round), take the steep climb up to the left, the Opal Canyon Trail. These trails are not marked but are easy to navigate. For about a half mile, it will follow an old roadbed. It gets very rocky in places with some cliffside exposure.

2.3 The trail forks here at a post. It's fainter to the left, but I recommend taking the left to do this outer loop in a clockwise fashion. It's rocky!

3.5 Stop for some awesome views of Lake Billy Chinook and the Crooked River Gorge.

4.6 You are back at the intersection where the trail forked. Stay straight.

5.1 At this intersection, take Otter Bench Trail back to the parking lot. Or take the Horny Hollow Trail back if it is open.

6.8 Return to your car at the Otter Bench trailhead.

WEST OF BEND AND WANOGA

The rides west of Bend are the trails that put Bend on the mountain biking map and can be accessed right from town. When you hear locals say that they rode "up at Phil's," they are referring to the triangle-shaped chunk of forest that is bordered by Skyliners Road to the north and Cascade Lakes Scenic Byway to the south, and extends up to the Swampy Lakes area. You can also connect to higher elevation trails from this trail network. Many of the trails have people names, and most of them refer to the intrepid early mountain bikers who built those trails. There are also funky, iconic landmarks to be found—a "flaming chicken" roundabout, modeled after the one on the west side of Bend, the Whoops bench, and the Helipad, rumored to be a helicopter landing site.

While the Phil's area trails are historic, previously renegade trails, the Wanoga complex, on the other hand, is the result of careful planning on the part of the Central Oregon Trail Alliance (COTA). In the early 2000s, as mountain biking in Bend was growing and becoming a destination activity, COTA and the Deschutes National Forest deemed that the Phil's Trail network wasn't a sustainable option for the increased amount of ridership or for organized races. The Wanoga network was funded through an Oregon State Recreation Trails Program (RTP) grant, and construction began in 2008. The final touches were put on the Catch and Release Trail in 2015. These trails are an incredible addition to Bend's mountain biking, and the two areas combined, Phil's and Wanoga, boast over 80 miles of singletrack. You

Opposite: *Trailside viewpoint on Mrazek*

One-way trails allow for uninterrupted climbing and descending in popular areas like the Phil's network.

can spend an hour or several days exploring this area.

Situated on the gently sloping east side of the Cascades, the Phil's Trail network and the Wanoga complex wind through dry pine trees and some mixed conifer forests at higher elevations. The majority of these trails are buffed out and fast, and if you catch them right after a strong summer rain spell, you'll have good traction, so pedal hard and hang on in the corners. However, in the heat of summer, they can get *very* dusty and loose in places. Some trails, specifically COD and Grand Slam in the Phil's network and parts of Funner in the Wanoga complex, are more technical, with stretches of sharp lava rock. Note that numerous dirt roads crisscross the trails in the Phil's network and the Wanoga complex. I have not included every road crossing in the route descriptions, only the trail intersections.

There are several races that occur on the Wanoga trails. Check with a local bike shop for race schedules so you don't get caught up there with racers flying past you. Parking at Phil's trailhead has become quite crowded over the years, so I recommend riding from town if you can. There are bike paths that parallel Skyliners Road so you don't have to ride the road. You'll save gas and money, do your part for clean air, and get a nice little warm-up before you hit the trails. And you can just ride back to a brewery of choice.

Speaking of food and drink, Bend has a large number of fabulous breweries, restaurants, and cafes that will satisfy you after a long day of pedaling. Many of them are on the west side of town and close to the trails.

6 PHIL'S CANYON

LOOP

Trail Type: 95% singletrack,
5% dirt road
Distance: 16.2 miles
Elevation Gain/Loss: 1350/1350 feet
High Point: 5057 feet
Ride Time: 2–3 hours
Technical Difficulty: Intermediate

Fitness Intensity: Moderate
Season: May–October
Map: Adventure Maps, Bend,
Oregon Trail Map
GPS: 44.0435° N, -121.3856° W
Land Manager: Deschutes National
Forest

OVERVIEW

If you sit in a pub in Bend, there is a good chance you'll overhear someone mention Phil's Trail. It is an iconic trail and the birthplace of singletrack mountain biking in central Oregon. This almost all-singletrack loop is a suggested route that includes a variety of trails in the network: gentle and steep hills, some technical challenges, and a mix of older, hand-built singletrack and more robust, machine-built trails with rollers, jumps, and berms.

Ben's Trail is designated for uphill riding only, and Lower Whoops Trail and the Phil's Canyon section of Phil's Trail are both downhill-only trails, meaning that you get to enjoy both uninterrupted climbing and ripping-fun descents. Practice the Trail Love principles—look, listen, and smile—in this popular area!

GETTING THERE

From the intersection of NE 3rd Street and NE Greenwood Avenue in Bend, take Greenwood Avenue west. In 1.5 miles, at the roundabout, turn left to head south on NW 14th Street. In 0.4 mile, turn right at the "flaming chicken" roundabout onto Galveston Avenue. Head west on Galveston Avenue (Skyliners Road), and in 2.7 miles turn left onto Forest Road 4604, continuing 0.5 mile to Phil's trailhead.

MILEAGE LOG

0.0 From Phil's trailhead, take Ben's Trail—the one farthest to your right if you are looking at the four trails. The first few miles include mostly

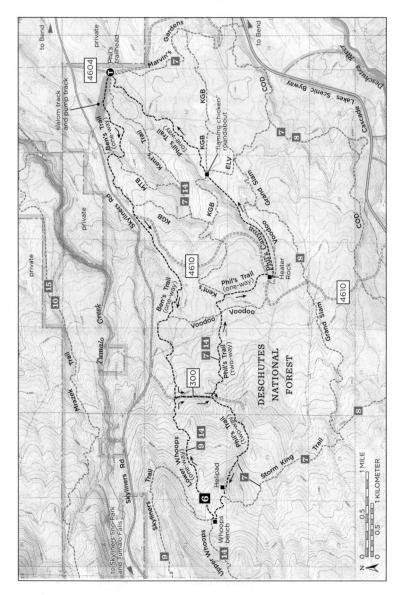

gentle uphill with some steeper pitches through an open pine forest.

1.3 Stay straight on Ben's Trail. Left will take you on MTB (locals call this Bealman's) for a much shorter loop.

2.3 KGB takes off to the left. Stay on Ben's Trail.

3.8 The trail splits for a very short section here. Ride to the left and you can challenge yourself on a technical, rocky up, or head right for an easy and smooth ride. At the top, you'll reach the intersection with Voodoo Trail. Stay straight on Ben's Trail. *Option: Turn left on Voodoo to get to Phil's Trail for a shorter loop.*

6.0 Turn left on FR 300, the "red road," for a quick down, then up.

6.5 Phil's Trail crosses your route here. It's the trail you see first to your left, and then a few feet ahead on your right. Take

The Phil's Canyon section of trail is one of the oldest mountain bike trails in Bend. (Photo: Chris Kratsch)

the trail to the right to ride up to the Helipad. The climb gets steep and technical in places, with switchbacks, tree roots, and a very short hike through some rocks. Pay attention on this two-way trail!

8.2 You've made it to the Helipad, the high point of the ride. From here, it's a short, fun descent.

8.3 Right after the Helipad, you'll come to the intersection with Storm King Trail. Stay to the right to remain on Phil's Trail.

8.5 The Whoops bench marks the intersection of Phil's Trail with Upper Whoops Trail, Lower Whoops Trail, and Skyliners Trail. Unless you want to add more riding, take downhill-only Lower Whoops and prepare for a rolly, bermy, jumpy trail. If you aren't into catching air, you can roll all of it if you can keep your speed in check.

10.2 Turn right onto FR 300 to cut back to Phil's Trail.

10.7 This time, turn left onto Phil's Trail. The upper sections of Phil's include flat and fast tread, easy-to-roll-over rocks, and great sections to practice your cornering skills.

11.7 At the intersection with Voodoo Trail, stay straight on Phil's.

12.0 At the three-way intersection with Kent's Trail, stay right to continue on Phil's. This intersection is the beginning of the designated downhill-only portion of Phil's Trail. *Option: Kent's is a fun way down, too; but it is a two-way trail, so you might be stopping for uphill traffic.*

12.6 Cross FR 4610 at Heater Rock. You are now entering Phil's Canyon. The canyon narrows and includes some rocky and rooty drops and twisty sections. Watch out for loose, sandy corners in the summer.

14.3 At the "flaming chicken" roundabout, stay straight and continue on Phil's Trail. (True to Bend, even the trails have roundabouts!) Other options include KGB to the right, ELV to the far right, and KGB to the left.

16.2 You've made it back to Phil's trailhead. Wipe the grin off your face and head into town for a beer!

7   KENT'S AND COD

LOOP

Trail Type: 100% singletrack
Distance: 20.8 miles
Elevation Gain/Loss: 1500/1500 feet
High Point: 5057 feet
Ride Time: 2–3 hours
Technical Difficulty: Advanced
Fitness Intensity: Strenuous

Season: May–October
Map: Adventure Maps, Bend, Oregon Trail Map
GPS: 44.0435° N, -121.3856° W
Land Manager: Deschutes National Forest

OVERVIEW

This ride includes Kent's Trail, which is my favorite trail in the Phil's Trail network for its cruising corners and fun descents. COD is the most technically challenging trail in the Phil's network, with plenty of lava rock, so you'll get a good mix of tread. I prefer to do this loop in a counterclockwise fashion,

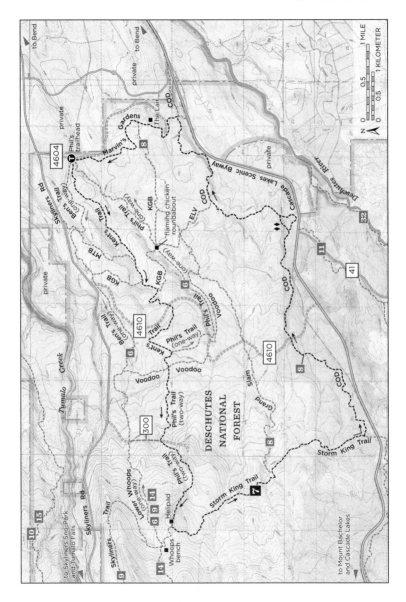

but it's really fun either way. If you choose to go the other direction, the climbing is significantly harder and more technical.

Unlike Ben's Trail and much of Phil's Trail, Kent's, Storm King, and COD are all two-way trails, so watch for oncoming traffic.

GETTING THERE

From the intersection of NE 3rd Street and NE Greenwood Avenue in Bend, take Greenwood Avenue west. In 1.5 miles, at the roundabout, turn left to head south on NW 14th Street. In 0.4 mile, turn right at the "flaming chicken" roundabout onto Galveston Avenue. Head west on Galveston Avenue (Skyliners Road), and in 2.7 miles turn left onto Forest Road 4604, continuing 0.5 mile to Phil's trailhead.

MILEAGE LOG

0.0 Start on Kent's Trail at Phil's trailhead. Kent's Trail is signed and is just to the left of Ben's Trail.

1.7 At the intersection with MTB Trail, stay straight on Kent's. As you ride up the canyon, the trail gets steeper and there are several splits in the trail. Don't worry, they all come back to the same place.

2.3 KGB takes off to the right here. Stay straight on Kent's.

2.5 At the second intersection with KGB, where it takes off to the left, continue on Kent's Trail.

4.0 At the three-way junction with Phil's Trail, turn right to get onto Phil's Trail.

4.3 Stay straight on Phil's Trail where Voodoo Trail crosses. *Option: If you turn left on Voodoo, you can take Grand Slam Trail (locally known as GS) back toward the trailhead, with a right on KGB and a left on Marvin's Gardens, for a shorter ride.*

5.3 At FR 300, continue on Phil's Trail. The trail starts just a little to the left of where you come out on the dirt road.

7.0 You're at the Helipad, the highest point on the ride and a great snack spot.

7.1 At the junction with Storm King Trail, take Storm King to the left.

9.0 After crossing a few dirt roads, you come to Grand Slam Trail. Continue straight/right on Storm King.

11.0 At the intersection with COD Trail, take a left onto COD. From here on, the trail roughly parallels Cascade Lakes Scenic Byway, which will be to your right in case you need a bailout point.

13.1 After crossing FR 4610, the trail becomes more technical, with lava rock outcroppings and tight corners for the next 2 miles.

15.1 You will see a split in the COD Trail. If you want a difficult "double black diamond" trail, stay to the left. If you go right, you will ride the easier trail. They both come back together eventually. Also, if you stay right, there is a spur that takes you to Cascade Lakes Scenic Byway, if you need to bail out onto the highway.

16.6 At ELV Trail, which goes to the left, stay straight on COD.

18.5 At the intersection with Marvin's Gardens, turn left onto Marvin's Gardens toward Phil's trailhead. COD will continue right and take you to Cascade Lakes Scenic Byway.

19.0 Watch for the sign for The Lair, a popular bike jumping playground. Stay on Marvin's Gardens.

19.3 At the intersection with KGB, continue straight.

20.8 Return to Phil's trailhead for the end of the ride.

Trails in the Phil's Trail network are well signed.

8 COD AND GRAND SLAM

LOOP

Trail Type: 100% singletrack
Distance: 20.7 miles
Elevation Gain/Loss: 1480/1480 feet
High Point: 4648 feet
Ride Time: 2–3 hours
Technical Difficulty: Advanced
Fitness Intensity: Strenuous

Season: May–October
Map: Adventure Maps, Bend, Oregon Trail Map
GPS: 44.0435° N, -121.3856° W
Land Manager: Deschutes National Forest

OVERVIEW

For the most part, many of the trails in the Phil's network are beginner friendly—they are smooth, wide, and fast with few technical sections. This ride, however, is the most technically challenging loop you can do in the Phil's Trail area. If you are looking for lava rock outcroppings, steeper climbs, and tighter singletrack, this is the ride for you. The elevation profile shows that it constantly rolls, up and down, keeping you on your toes. Watch out for riders going the opposite direction on all of these two-way trails.

Many of these trails don't get ridden as much as the other ones just to the north. COD has been here for decades, but has changed and has been rerouted over time due to the squeeze of private land and the building of new Forest Service facilities. Also, look for some trailside art along the way!

You may find this ride to be hard to navigate at times, simply because there are so many intersections and trail names. It will be helpful to have the Adventure Maps *Bend, Oregon Trail Map* with you to get your bearings.

GETTING THERE

From the intersection of NE 3rd Street and NE Greenwood Avenue in Bend, take Greenwood Avenue west. In 1.5 miles, at the roundabout, turn left to head south on NW 14th Street. In 0.4 mile, turn right at the "flaming chicken" roundabout onto Galveston Avenue. Head west on Galveston Avenue (Skyliners Road), and in 2.7 miles turn left onto Forest Road 4604, continuing 0.5 mile to Phil's trailhead.

MILEAGE LOG

0.0 At Phil's trailhead, take Marvin's Gardens, the farthest trail to the left. It will take you through open sage, a recent prescribed burn, and an old quarry, with up-and-down rollers. You'll encounter several splits in the trail, but you can choose either way as they all come back together eventually.

1.7 At a little overlook with a view of Bend through the trees, KGB Trail takes off to the right. Stay straight on Marvin's Gardens.

2.1 At the rough-cut sign for The Lair, the popular bike jumping playground, stay straight on Marvin's Gardens.

2.6 When you reach the junction with COD, stay right. This is where Marvin's turns into COD. Left will take you to Cascade Lakes Scenic Byway.

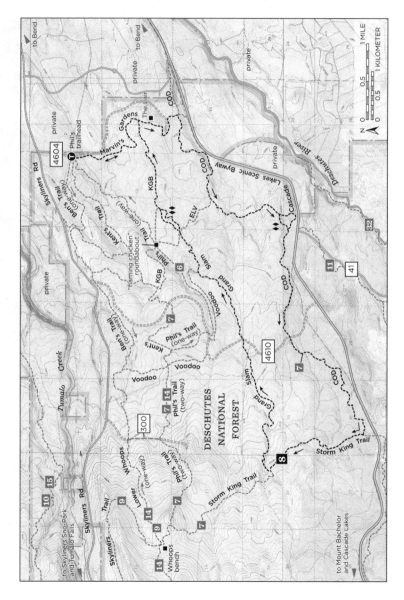

4.5 At the intersection with ELV Trail to the right, stay straight on COD.

6.0 COD Trail splits here, but will come back together. If you are looking for a challenging "double black diamond" route, stay to the right. Otherwise go left.

8.0 Cross FR 4610 here and stay straight on COD.

10.1 Upon reaching Storm King Trail, turn right. Cascade Lakes Scenic Byway is also nearby if you need a bailout point. Storm King continues to climb at a fairly mellow grade.

12.1 Look for a large clearing, where a few dirt roads and trails come together. Take a right on Grand Slam (locals refer to it as GS). This is also roughly the highest point on the ride.

Keep an eye out for trailside art in the Phil's Trail network.

15.7 At the intersection with Voodoo Trail to the left, stay straight/right on GS.

16.4 GS splits here and if you want the hard route, stay to the right. Otherwise, stay to the left for the easier route. Both ways have some rocks to negotiate, though.

17.1 When you reach this large intersection of trails, stay to the right to take KGB back to Marvin's Gardens.

19.0 At the intersection with Marvin's Gardens, turn left.

20.7 Return to Phil's trailhead.

9 TUMALO FALLS AND WHOOPS

OUT-AND-BACK

Trail Type: 90% singletrack, 10% dirt road
Distance: 17 miles
Elevation Gain/Loss: 940/940 feet
High Point: 5031 feet
Ride Time: 2–3 hours
Technical Difficulty: Intermediate

Fitness Intensity: Moderate
Season: June–October
Map: Adventure Maps, Bend, Oregon Trail Map
GPS: 44.0330° N, -121.4614° W
Land Manager: Deschutes National Forest

OVERVIEW

I've added this ride into the mix because no other ride in this book specifically includes Skyliners Trail, an important connector trail between the Phil's Trail network and the higher alpine trails that start in the Tumalo Creek valley. It's a nice ride for an intermediate rider due to its low elevation profile and fairly tame nature, and it takes you to Tumalo Falls. This is also a favorite after-work single-speed ride for me when I just want to get out and pedal fast for two hours. This route includes the classic Lower Whoops loop, so if you want to up your fun factor, take a few laps on this lower section.

You can see on the map that there are tons of options with connecting trails that can take you up or down in elevation. For example, you could explore additional trails in the Phil's Trail network, or you could fold this ride into a high alpine shuttle.

GETTING THERE

From the intersection of NE 3rd Street and NE Greenwood Avenue in Bend, take Greenwood Avenue west. In 1.5 miles, at the roundabout, turn left on NW 14th Street. In 0.4 mile, at the "flaming chicken" roundabout, turn right onto Galveston Avenue (Skyliners Road). In another 6.5 miles, turn left onto Forest Road 300. Drive a quarter mile down this dirt road and find a place

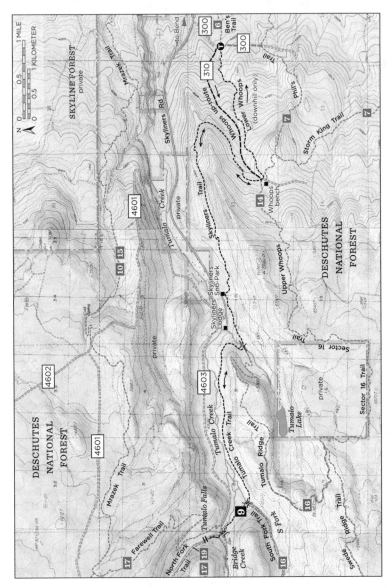

to park. This is a popular parking place, so you will likely see other cars parked along here.

MILEAGE LOG

0.0 From where you parked along FR 300, head to where you see Ben's Trail to the left and FR 310 to the right, which is the Whoops up-route. Turn right on FR 310.

1.9 You will reach the Whoops bench at the intersection of Lower Whoops Trail, Upper Whoops Trail, Phil's Trail, and Skyliners Trail. You will want to get on Skyliners Trail to the north. If you are looking at the bench, Skyliners Trail will be behind you. After a mellow climb up, enjoy a fun downhill that takes you to Skyliners Sno-Park.

5.1 At Skyliners Sno-Park, take the Tumalo Creek Trail, the trail just to the right of the outhouse.

The Tumalo Creek Trail follows the Tumalo Creek drainage. (Photo: Chris Kratsch)

5.7 Cross the creek on a wooden bridge.

5.8 At the intersection with the Tumalo Ridge Trail, stay right to follow the Tumalo Creek Trail. This two-way section of trail is popular with runners and hikers, so take caution on blind corners and use a bell if you have one.

8.1 After crossing Tumalo Creek on the bridge, turn right at the junction with the South Fork Trail to stay on the Tumalo Creek Trail. You will cross the creek once more before reaching the falls.

8.6 You are now at Tumalo Falls, and you have the option to ride up the short, but steep, pitch to the overlook to get a closer view of the impressive falls. From here, you'll turn around and go back the way you came.

9.1 Turn left at the intersection with South Fork Trail.

11.4 Turn left at the intersection with the Tumalo Ridge Trail, then cross the creek.

12.1 At Skyliners Sno-Park, take Skyliners Trail to ride back the way you came.

15.3 You are back at the four-way Whoops bench intersection. Now you get to finish the ride rolling (or jumping) Lower Whoops. Lower Whoops is a downhill-only trail. Whoop it up!

17.0 At the bottom of Lower Whoops, you can choose to ride the Whoops loop again, or head back to your car. The Whoops loop is a one-way loop, so you would hop on FR 310 again to ride back up to the Whoops bench, then back down the trail.

10 MRAZEK

OUT-AND-BACK

Trail Type: 100% singletrack
Distance: 32.2 miles
Elevation Gain/Loss: 2910/2910 feet
High Point: 6234 feet
Ride Time: 1–5 hours
Technical Difficulty: Intermediate
Fitness Intensity: Moderate–very strenuous

Season: May–October
Map: Adventure Maps, Bend, Oregon Trail Map
GPS: 44.0826° N, -121.3778° W
Land Managers: Deschutes National Forest; Bend Park and Recreation District

OVERVIEW

Mrazek Trail is a rather historic mountain biking trail, named after Mrazek Cycles, a then Bend-based bike frame builder that started building bicycles in the late 1980s. Ridden out and back in entirety, this ride is 32.2 miles, skirting the ridges to the north of Tumalo Creek. It also borders Skyline Forest, which includes over 30,000 acres of privately owned land that reaches almost to the town of Sisters. If you are interested in the future of Skyline Forest, check out the Deschutes Land Trust at www.deschuteslandtrust.org, as they are working to preserve much of the land for multiple recreational uses, including mountain biking.

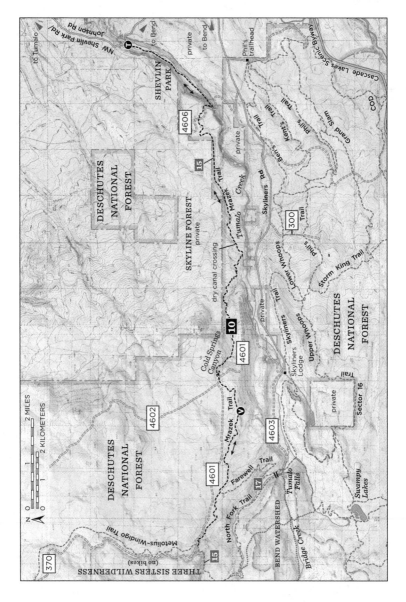

Mrazek Trail sign

This ride starts in Shevlin Park, a 652-acre suburban park just west of Bend. The park is very popular with runners, hikers, dog walkers, and school groups, so don't be alarmed if it seems crowded when you get there. As with other trails, the higher you get, the fewer people you will see.

Mrazek is noted as having tight and twisty trails with some close calls with trees. It follows a gradual but consistent climb up. This trail is also unique for the area because there really aren't any options or other connecting trails until you get really high up in elevation. There, you can access other trails such as Farewell Trail and Metolius–Windigo. Higher reaches of this trail are accessible only in midsummer to late summer, when the snow is melted and the downed trees are cut out.

The fitness intensity rating for this ride is moderate to very strenuous, simply because this is an out-and-back trail and you can turn around whenever you like. The farther you go, the more strenuous the ride is.

GETTING THERE

From the intersection of NE 3rd Street and NE Greenwood Avenue in Bend, drive west on Greenwood Avenue for 4.5 miles until you reach Shevlin Park (Greenwood Avenue eventually becomes NW Shevlin Park Road). Shevlin

Park is at the bottom of the hill when you cross Tumalo Creek. The park is on both sides of the road. Park your vehicle on the left side of the park; the right side is reserved for Aspen Hall, a popular spot for weddings and other events.

MILEAGE LOG

0.0 Start in Shevlin Park by taking the trail to the right, just beyond the caretaker's house. Follow this trail above the paved park road and Tumalo Creek.

2.5 Take the trail hard right to climb out of Shevlin Park. You'll encounter some switchbacks and rocky sections.

3.3 When you reach FR 4606, continue straight across onto Mrazek and get settled into a very consistent, but fairly low-grade climb on this two-way trail. There are some tight corners, so keep an eye and ear out for oncoming mountain bike traffic.

6.9 At the dry canal, continue straight across on Mrazek.

10.2 Upon entering a large clearing and intersection of dirt roads, you'll continue on the trail up Cold Springs Canyon. From here, the trail becomes a bit steeper, with some loose rocks.

12.2 Look to the left and you'll find a trail that leads to a nice viewpoint that overlooks the Tumalo Creek valley.

14.6 At the intersection with Farewell Trail, to your left, stay on Mrazek.

16.1 At the wide intersection of FR 4601, FR 370, and Metolius–Windigo Trail, Mrazek Trail officially ends, so this is the turnaround point to go back to Shevlin Park. *Option: If you want to add on an epic loop, you can take Metolius–Windigo Trail to the left (southwest) all the way to Flagline Trail, South Fork Trail, and Farewell Trail back to Mrazek. Expect a ton of climbing and a very long day.*

17.6 Continue on Mrazek Trail when you see Farewell Trail spurring off to the right.

22.0 At the bottom of Cold Springs Canyon, continue on Mrazek. Farther down Mrazek, you will see a split in the trail, with the trail to the left signed as "double black diamond." I recommend following this trail to the left. It's not really "double black diamond," but it is a really swoopy route down an old canal, and though not very challenging, it will have you grinning.

28.9 At FR 4606, ride straight across to begin descending to Shevlin Park.

29.7 At the hard left, take the singletrack trail back through Shevlin Park toward the parking lot where you started the ride. *Option: If you are whipped and* *ready to be done, you can take the wider, flatter trail near the creek. This will eventually turn to pavement and bring you back to the parking lot.*

32.2 Finish the ride back at Shevlin Park.

11 FUNNER AND TIDDLYWINKS

LOOP

Trail Type: 100% singletrack
Distance: 23.9 miles
Elevation Gain/Loss: 2310/2310 feet
High Point: 5554 feet
Ride Time: 3–4 hours
Technical Difficulty: Intermediate
Fitness Intensity: Strenuous

Season: June–October
Map: Adventure Maps, Bend, Oregon Trail Map
GPS: 43.9972° N, -121.4041° W
Land Manager: Deschutes National Forest

OVERVIEW

This ride includes one of Bend's newest trails, Catch and Release, which connects Cascade Lakes Scenic Byway to the lower elevation terminus of the Wanoga trails. The full trail is 4.8 miles from the highway to Tyler's Traverse (Route 12). For this loop, you'll take Catch and Release to Storm King. Prior to the creation of this trail, we had to ride paved Forest Road 41 to connect lower Tyler's and Storm King and the highway. Thanks to COTA and dedicated volunteers, we can now ride singletrack the whole way.

This loop includes a mix of trails. Storm King is an older, more traditionally built singletrack trail; Funner is a mix of technical, rocky tread and fast and smooth sections. The middle of Tiddlywinks is one of the few machine-built flow trails that we have in the Bend area, with big, sweeping corners, tabletop jumps, and rolling terrain. These trails can get dusty in the middle of summer, so watch for loose, blown-out corners in spots. All of these trails are also two-way trails, so watch for oncoming traffic.

Note that the technical difficulty for this ride is shown as intermediate, but there are a few short sections of more advanced trail, particularly on Funner.

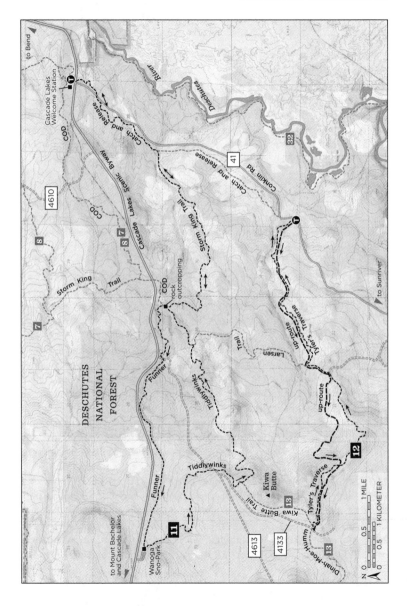

GETTING THERE

This ride starts at the Deschutes National Forest Cascade Lakes Welcome Station on Cascade Lakes Scenic Byway. From the intersection of NE 3rd Street and NE Greenwood Avenue in Bend, take Greenwood Avenue west. In 1.5 miles, at the roundabout, turn left to head south on NW 14th Street. At the "flaming chicken" roundabout, stay straight to continue on NW 14th Street, which eventually becomes Cascade Lakes Scenic Byway. In another 6.7 miles, just past Forest Road 41, look for the Forest Service welcome center on the right. Park here.

MILEAGE LOG

0.0 From the welcome center parking lot, carefully cross Cascade Lakes Scenic Byway to start on Catch and Release. (The Forest Service has plans to build a tunnel for the trail to go under the highway, which will be a much nicer alternative to crossing the highway.)

0.5 Cross FR 41.

2.0 At the intersection with Storm King Trail, turn right on Storm King. You'll gradually climb up Storm King, crossing a few dirt roads along the way.

6.2 At the four-way intersection, near the big rock pile, take the second left on Funner Trail. Make a note of this intersection for when you return later on.

6.3 As soon as you get on Funner, you'll notice an "up-route" and a "down-route." Take the up-route. There are more sections like this as you continue climbing. Funner is a two-way trail, but trail builders have conveniently constructed specific two-lane sections to avoid conflict, so be sure to take the up-route.

10.7 Wanoga Sno-Park is your turnaround point. There is a pump track here, a short, looping trail system with berms and rollers—perfect for skill building. Take a spin on it if you need some extra fun! From here, take Tiddlywinks Trail, which starts to the right of the warming hut.

13.7 At the intersection with the Kiwa Butte Trail, stay left on Tiddlywinks. From here, it is easy to gain speed quickly; watch for oncoming traffic, as this is a two-way trail. *Option: If you take Kiwa Butte Trail, you can catch Tyler's Traverse (see Route 12) as an alternative descent.*

16.9 At the intersection with the Larsen Trail to the right, stay straight on Tiddlywinks. You will cross FR 4130 just past this intersection.

Funner is funner! (Photo: Cog Wild)

17.7 Now you are back at that four-way intersection with Funner and Storm King. Note that Storm King also connects with COD here, which continues over to Cascade Lakes Scenic Byway. If you need a bailout point, this is it. Otherwise, you'll want to continue on Storm King back down the way you came.

21.9 At the intersection with Catch and Release, turn left. You will ride parallel to FR 41 again, so if you want to hit the pavement, now's your chance.

23.9 Return to Cascade Lakes Scenic Byway and cross (safely!) back to the welcome center.

The meadow section on Tyler's Traverse is fast and flowy.

12 TYLER'S TRAVERSE

LOOP

Trail Type: 60% singletrack, 40% dirt road

Distance: 12.8 miles

Elevation Gain/Loss: 2340/2340 feet

High Point: 5567 feet

Ride Time: 1–3 hours

Technical Difficulty: Intermediate

Fitness Intensity: Strenuous

Season: June–October

Map: Adventure Maps, Bend, Oregon Trail Map

GPS: 43.9530° N, -121.4436° W

Land Manager: Deschutes National Forest

OVERVIEW

Tyler's Traverse is one of my favorite early morning or after-work summer rides, especially after some rain, when the trail is tacky and fast. In midsummer to late summer it can get loose and dusty, but is still a whooping good time. As a designated one-way loop, it follows a series of old dirt roads for the uphill route, and 100 percent singletrack on the way down. This provides for a nice two-hour ride with a consistent climb and a fast descent, and once you see how fast you can go on the downhill, you'll be thankful for the one-way rule. The route is also well signed for the uphill and downhill portions.

For the route map, see Route 11, Funner and Tiddlywinks.

GETTING THERE

From the intersection of NE 3rd Street and NE Greenwood Avenue in Bend, take Greenwood Avenue west. In 1.5 miles, at the roundabout, turn left to head south on NW 14th Street. At the "flaming chicken" roundabout, stay straight to continue on NW 14th Street, which eventually becomes the Cascade Lakes Scenic Byway. In another 6.7 miles, turn left onto Forest Road 41 (Conklin Road). The parking area for Tyler's Traverse will be in 3.8 miles on the right.

MILEAGE LOG

0.0 Starting at the trailhead, you'll see three signed trails right next to each other. Take the steep trail up to the far left to begin the up-route for this ride.

0.2 At the dirt road, turn right and climb. You'll see the trail cross the road in about another half mile, but stay on the road, which will vary in steepness.

2.5 The route in this section makes a series of turns, all on dirt roads, some of which have become narrow due to the restrictions on cars on the roads. These are all well signed as "Uphill Route," so continue to follow those signs.

4.3 Here, the route veers to the left and narrows and steepens as you climb up.

5.1 When you reach another trail crossing, stay straight on the road. *Option: For a shorter ride, you can turn left on the trail here and start downhill. Don't turn right onto the trail, as this is a one-way downhill trail and you'll be going the wrong way.*

6.0 Take the right onto the Tyler's Traverse down-route. You'll climb a short hill right away that will put you at the highest point of the ride. The first third of the mostly downhill singletrack has a few short, steep climbs and some rock gardens. *Option: For a longer ride, stay straight on the Kiwa Butte Trail and add an out-and-back section, or turn left onto Dinah-Moe-Humm for another out-and-back option.*

7.3 After crossing the up-route dirt road, you'll ride over and through lava rock boulders with some very steep uphill pitches. After the second steep rock ramp, it really is all downhill from there!

9.5 At the intersection with the Larsen Trail, which takes off to the left, you will want to stay on Tyler's. All road crossings are obvious and signed from here. *Option: The Larsen Trail will take you north over to Tiddlywinks (see Route 11).*

12.8 Wipe the grin off from that screaming descent, and go do it again if you have some juice left!

OPTIONS

Start instead at the Cascade Lakes Welcome Station at the intersection of Cascade Lakes Scenic Byway and FR 41. Take the very new Catch and Release Trail to add on 9.6 miles roundtrip (see Route 11, Funner and Tiddlywinks).

13 WANOGA TO DINAH-MOE-HUMM

OUT-AND-BACK

Trail Type: 100% singletrack
Distance: 21 miles
Elevation Gain/Loss: 1900/1900 feet
High Point: 5643 feet
Ride Time: 2–4 hours
Technical Difficulty: Advanced
Fitness Intensity: Strenuous

Season: July–October
Map: Adventure Maps, Bend, Oregon Trail Map
GPS: 43.9828° N, -121.5359° W
Land Manager: Deschutes National Forest

OVERVIEW

Wanoga Sno-Park is the starting point for this out-and-back ride that includes the Kiwa Butte Trail and Dinah-Moe-Humm Trail. Many people shuttle from Wanoga to town, or ride both trails as a loop from the bottom of Storm King or Tyler's Traverse. I've added in this alternative route because it is an out-and-back ride that includes lonely trails that take you through

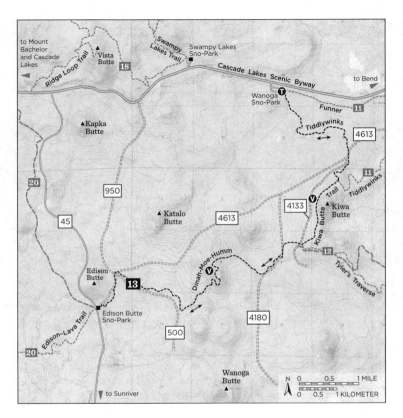

lovely mixed conifer forests with occasional scenic views of Mount Bachelor and the Cascade mountains. The lowest elevation point on this ride is at the midway turnaround point at Forest Road 45, so be prepared to "keep on climbing" for the second half of the ride.

GETTING THERE

From the intersection of NE 3rd Street and NE Greenwood Avenue in Bend, take Greenwood Avenue west. In 1.5 miles, at the roundabout, turn left to head south on NW 14th Street. At the "flaming chicken" roundabout, stay

A sneak peek of Mount Bachelor through the trees on the Kiwa Butte Trail (Photo: Chris Kratsch)

straight to continue on NW 14th Street, which eventually becomes the Cascade Lakes Scenic Byway. In another 14 miles, turn left into Wanoga Sno-Park. Park in the farthest east parking lot, near the pump track.

MILEAGE LOG

0.0 From the east end of the parking lot, take Tiddlywinks Trail, just past the restrooms. As you ride along, you'll encounter several places where the trail splits into alternate routes. Most of these are signed, and some are designated as green (easy), blue (more difficult), and black (most difficult). In each instance you can choose which way you want to go, as they all come back together into one trail eventually.

3.0 At the intersection of Tiddlywinks and Kiwa Butte Trail, continue straight on Kiwa Butte Trail.

3.4 Need a break? There's a nice log bench with a view of Mount Bachelor here, a perfect spot for a snack.

4.4 At the junction with Tyler's Traverse and Dinah-Moe-Humm, take Dinah-Moe-Humm to the right.

4.6 At FR 4180, continue straight across on Dinah-Moe-Humm.

5.9 You'll start a steeper climb up to another butte, where you'll be rewarded with more nice views of the mountains. From this viewpoint, it is mostly downhill to paved FR 45 and Edison Butte Sno-Park.

10.0 When you encounter the large intersection of FR 500, FR 950, and FR 4613, look for the trail crossing and continue on Dinah-Moe-Humm.

10.5 At paved FR 45, turn around and head back the way you came on Dinah-Moe-Humm. *Option: Edison Butte Sno-Park is on the other side of the road. From it, you can find the Edison–Lava Trail on the other side of the parking lot and take this all the way to Lava Lake. Expect steep climbs and challenging conditions.*

16.6 At the intersection with Tyler's Traverse and Kiwa Butte Trail, take Kiwa Butte Trail to the left.

17.6 You're back at the log bench on Kiwa Butte and done with climbing. Yippee! Now it really is downhill to the car.

18.0 At the Tiddlywinks Trail intersection, turn left.

21.0 Return to Wanoga Sno-Park for the end of the ride.

HIGH
CASCADES

Summertime is the peak season for mountain biking in Bend, mainly because the snow at the higher elevations starts melting, opening up more miles of singletrack for the summer months. The High Cascades area is considered to be everything above Swampy Lakes Sno-Park (elevation 5800 feet), on both sides of Cascade Lakes Scenic Byway.

In the summer, when the heat turns on in Bend, locals head for the hills to experience cooler temperatures and enjoy more opportunities to be near water, such as rocky creeks and alpine lakes. Right around 5000 feet elevation, the drier ponderosa pine forest transitions into more mixed forest with a variety of firs, spruces, white pines, and hemlocks. Some of these rides, such as parts of the Metolius–Windigo Trail, Swede Ridge, Farewell Trail, and Vista Butte, have great views of Mount Bachelor, Tumalo Mountain, and Broken Top. The forests are interspersed with wide alpine meadows throughout, making for nice places to have a snack, photo op, or even a mid-ride nap.

The trails can still be sandy in places, with occasional loose volcanic pumice, but some trails have a nice layer of duff (organic matter). A few of these rides start at Dutchman Flat, which is a large, flat pumice field. Although it may look like it is a bit of a dead zone, there are tiny, fragile plants that live on the pumice, so don't ride off-trail here.

Depending on the harshness and snowpack of the previous winter, some of the lower trails near Swampy Lakes Sno-Park can open up as early as May, but the higher elevation trails might not open until mid- to late August. Flagline Trail does not open until August 15 every year because it is closed and protected until then as critical elk calving habitat. Please don't ride this trail until the closure ends!

Opposite: *Riders bomb down a fast section of the Metolius–Windigo Trail.*
(Photo: Cog Wild)

14 DUTCHMAN TO FLAGLINE TO PHIL'S

SHUTTLE

Trail Type: 95% singletrack, 5% dirt road
Distance: 22.1 miles
Elevation Gain/Loss: 1140/3610 feet
High Point: 6970 feet
Ride Time: 4–5 hours
Technical Difficulty: Advanced
Fitness Intensity: Strenuous

Season: August 15–October
Map: Adventure Maps, Bend, Oregon Trail Map
GPS: Start: 43.9997° N, -121.6658° W; End: 44.0435° N, -121.3856° W
Land Manager: Deschutes National Forest

OVERVIEW

This popular shuttle offers a full Oregon Cascades singletrack experience, taking you from the base of Mount Bachelor to Phil's trailhead. Starting in cool alpine fir and hemlock forest and ending in the pine trees of the Phil's Trail network, you'll cover a lot of ground through forests, alpine meadows, wildflowers, and creek crossings, with the potential for spotting wildlife.

Flagline Trail is a landmark trail and local favorite in central Oregon with flowing corners, fast descents, and a handful of log rides. However, it doesn't open until August 15 every year because it runs through important elk calving habitat. Remember that we share the trails with other species, so please respect the closure until August 15.

Be warned—even though this is a shuttle ride that has a net elevation loss, there are some uphills. This is why I've listed the ride as strenuous. Be prepared to pedal all day, and make sure to take breaks and shake the legs out at the three ski shelters you'll pass along the way. I've included Sector 16 Trail on this ride, and it is a noticeably different trail that is very twisty and tight in a forest of downed logs. The route as I've written it up takes you back to Phil's trailhead via Kent's Trail, but there are many options once you enter the Phil's Trail network.

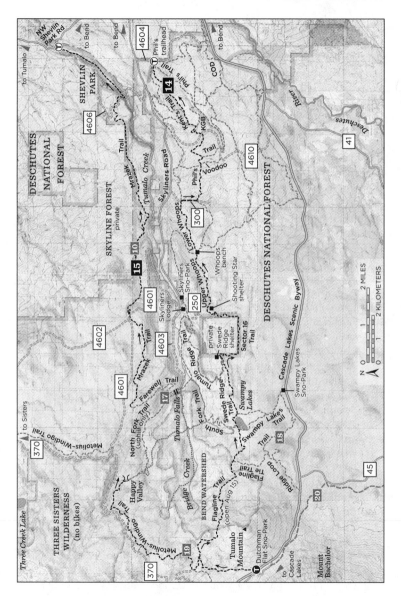

GETTING THERE

To reach the start of the ride at Dutchman Flat Sno-Park: From the intersection of NE 3rd Street and NE Greenwood Avenue in Bend, take Greenwood Avenue west. In 1.5 miles, at the roundabout, turn left to head south on NW 14th Street. At the "flaming chicken" roundabout, stay straight to continue on NW 14th Street, which eventually becomes Cascade Lakes Scenic Byway. At 20.8 miles, turn right into Dutchman Flat Sno-Park and park here.

To reach the end of the ride at Phil's trailhead: From the intersection of NE 3rd Street and NE Greenwood Avenue in Bend, take Greenwood Avenue west. In 1.5 miles, at the roundabout, turn left to head south on NW 14th Street. In 0.4 mile, turn right at the "flaming chicken" roundabout onto Galveston Avenue. Head west on Galveston Avenue (Skyliners Road). In 2.7 miles, turn left on Forest Road 4604 and continue 0.5 mile to Phil's trailhead.

MILEAGE LOG

0.0 At Dutchman Flat Sno-Park, take the trail that starts to the right of the outhouse. This trail takes you along the west flank of Tumalo Mountain, with Dutchman Flat to your left.

2.2 At the intersection with Flagline Trail, turn right. From here, you will start climbing for about a mile, then descend. This is technically a two-way trail, so keep an eye out for uphill riders.

6.1 At the intersection with Flagline Tie Trail, stay straight on Flagline, a ripping-fun section of trail.

7.2 You are now in the Swampy Lakes area. Stay straight/left on the Swampy Lakes Trail.

7.8 Turn left on Swede Ridge Trail.

9.8 You'll pop out onto a dirt road. Down to the left is the Swede Ridge shelter, and straight ahead is Sector 16 Trail. Take Sector 16 Trail, which hugs private land; please stay on the trail. Also, watch out for dead and downed trees, as this is a thick, rather unhealthy portion of forest that tends to see a lot of blowdown from windstorms.

13.3 Cross FR 250.

13.5 At the Shooting Star shelter, take Upper Whoops Trail. You'll cross a few dirt roads, but stay on Upper Whoops.

14.9 You have reached the Whoops bench at the intersection of Upper Whoops, Skyliners Trail, Lower Whoops Trail, and Phil's Trail. Go straight to get on Lower Whoops. *Option: Alternatively, you can take*

Phil's to Storm King and GS or COD (see Routes 7 and 8), or you can take Phil's to the Helipad and continue on Phil's (see Route 6).

16.6 At the bottom of Lower Whoops, turn right on FR 300.

17.0 At Phil's Trail, turn left.

18.0 At the Voodoo Trail crossing, stay straight on Phil's.

18.3 At the three-way intersection of Phil's and Kent's Trail, turn left on Kent's Trail.

19.8 When you reach the junction where KGB Trail goes to the right, stay straight on Kent's. Soon after, KGB will take off to the left, but you will continue on Kent's.

20.4 At the intersection with MTB Trail to the left, stay straight on Kent's.

22.1 End the ride at Phil's trailhead.

Sweet, sweet singletrack

15 DUTCHMAN TO METOLIUS–WINDIGO TO SHEVLIN PARK

SHUTTLE

Trail Type: 100% singletrack
Distance: 25.6 miles
Elevation Gain/Loss: 1280/4010 feet
High Point: 6870 feet
Ride Time: 4–6 hours
Technical Difficulty: Advanced
Fitness Intensity: Strenuous
Season: August–October

Map: Adventure Maps, Bend, Oregon Trail Map
GPS: Start: 43.9997° N, -121.6658° W; End: 44.0826° N, -121.3778° W
Land Managers: Deschutes National Forest; Bend Park and Recreation District

OVERVIEW

If you are looking for a multihour ride that covers a lot of ground and offers a ton of variety, this route fits the bill. Although it is known as a downhill shuttle and there is a net elevation loss, there is still a fair amount of pedaling, so prepare for a substantial ride to tick off your checklist. This section of the Metolius–Windigo Trail is one of my favorite trails in these parts, with fun creek crossings, meadows, and mountain views.

This ride starts at Dutchman Flat Sno-Park, across the road from the base of Mount Bachelor, and heads north through nice High Cascades alpine terrain, eventually crossing Tumalo Creek. From there, Mrazek Trail is more than 11 miles of uninterrupted singletrack, ending at Shevlin Park. There aren't many bailout points along this ride, especially once you get on

Crossing the creek on the Metolius–Windigo Trail (Photo: Cog Wild)

Mrazek, so be prepared with adequate supplies, food, and water for a solid day in the saddle.

For the route map, see Route 14, Dutchman to Flagline to Phil's.

GETTING THERE

To reach the start of the ride at Dutchman Flat Sno-Park: From the intersection of NE 3rd Street and NE Greenwood Avenue in Bend, take Greenwood Avenue west. In 1.5 miles, at the roundabout, turn left to head south on NW 14th Street. At the "flaming chicken" roundabout, stay straight to continue on NW 14th Street, which eventually becomes Cascade Lakes Scenic Byway. At 20.8 miles, turn right into Dutchman Flat Sno-Park and park here.

To reach the end of the ride at Shevlin Park: From the intersection of NE 3rd Street and NE Greenwood Avenue in Bend, drive west on Greenwood Avenue for 4.5 miles until you reach Shevlin Park (Greenwood Avenue eventually becomes NW Shevlin Park Road). It is at the bottom of the hill when you cross Tumalo Creek. Park in the parking lot on the left side of the road; the right side is reserved for Aspen Hall, a popular spot for weddings and other events.

MILEAGE LOG

0.0 At Dutchman Flat Sno-Park, take the trail that starts to the right of the outhouse. This trail will take you along the west flank of Tumalo Mountain, with Dutchman Flat to your left.

2.2 At the intersection with Flagline Trail, turn left.

2.9 Stay far right at this intersection to get on the Metolius–Windigo Trail. The two trails to the left head toward FR 370 and Todd Lake. Ride north on Metolius–Windigo to enjoy some pretty alpine meadows, creek crossings, and views of Broken Top Mountain.

5.2 Stay straight here. The short spur to the left goes to FR 370 if you need a bailout point.

8.4 At Happy Valley, turn left to cross the creek on the bridge and stay on Metolius–Windigo Trail. To the right is North Fork Trail, but mountain bikes are not allowed to ride downhill on this uphill-only trail.

9.5 After riding parallel to FR 370 for about a mile, you'll reach the intersection of FR 370 and FR 4601. Here, you will take Mrazek Trail to the east.

11.0   Farewell Trail (which ends at Tumalo Falls) takes off to the right. Stay on Mrazek. From here, you'll stay on Mrazek for the long haul. It varies in nature, with some steeper sections in Cold Springs Canyon and some flatter, winding sections as you drop in elevation. *Option: Take Farewell Trail down to Tumalo Creek and Tumalo Falls to eventually access Skyliners Trail and the Phil's Trail network.*

22.3   Cross FR 4606. You are now just above Shevlin Park. You'll descend into the park, encountering a few rocky switchbacks along the way. At the last switchback that turns left, when you are near Tumalo Creek, stay left.

23.2   Here you can choose to stay on the west (left) side of the creek or cross the creek on the footbridge to the right. The easier and flatter route is to stay on the west side of the creek and the harder and steeper route is on the other side of the river. Take either trail back to the main parking area at Shevlin Park.

25.6   Reach the main parking area at Shevlin Park for the end of the ride.

16   SWEDE RIDGE AND SOUTH FORK

LOOP

Trail Type: 85% singletrack, 15% dirt road

Distance: 13.3 miles

Elevation Gain/Loss: 1590/1590 feet

High Point: 5924 feet

Ride Time: 1.5–2.5 hours

Technical Difficulty: Advanced

Fitness Intensity: Moderate

Season: June–October

Map: Adventure Maps, Bend, Oregon Trail Map

GPS: 44.0315° N, -121.5150° W

Land Manager: Deschutes National Forest

OVERVIEW

This loop is another local favorite, for the Bend rider who wants a quick early morning or late-afternoon ride with a solid climb, fun downhill, and a stop at a ski shelter with commanding views of Broken Top and the Tumalo Creek valley. The ski shelters up here are primarily used as wintertime

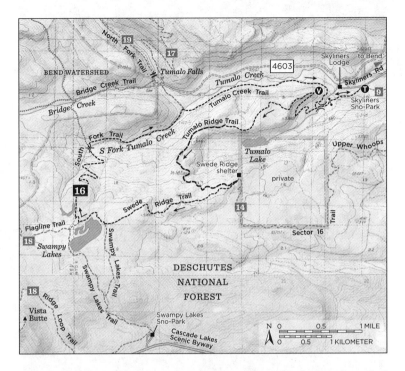

warming huts; but they offer a nice reprieve from bad weather if you find yourself up here in a storm.

The first half of the ride climbs Tumalo Ridge Trail, also known to some riders as Rockless Ridge (it is not rockless), then continues up to the Swede Ridge shelter and Swampy Lakes Sno-Park area. The South Fork Trail is a classic downhill with the potential for speed, intermixed with big roots, switchbacks, and body-thumping water bars. South Fork Trail also skirts the Bend Watershed, the water supply for all of Bend. Don't do anything bad around there, or all of Bend will be drinking it.

GETTING THERE

From the intersection of NE 3rd Street and NE Greenwood Avenue in Bend, take Greenwood Avenue west. In 1.5 miles, at the roundabout, turn left to

South Fork Trail is a ripping-fun descent through the trees. (Photo: Cog Wild)

head south on NW 14th Street. In 0.4 mile, at the "flaming chicken" round-about, turn right onto Galveston Avenue and head west on what will become Skyliners Road. In 9.7 miles, you'll reach Skyliners Sno-Park on the left. Please watch your speed while driving out here, as this is a quiet neighborhood with a lot of kids and dogs.

MILEAGE LOG

0.0 Start at Skyliners Sno-Park on the Tumalo Creek Trail to the right of the kiosk and the outhouse.

0.5 Continue through the green gate.

0.6 Cross the creek on a wooden bridge.

0.7 At the intersection of Tumalo Creek Trail and Tumalo Ridge Trail, take the left onto Tumalo Ridge Trail for a quick switchback, then traverse up the hillside.

1.5 Enjoy the nice view of the Tumalo Creek valley. The trail gets steeper and rockier here, and in the heat of summer it can be hot and dusty.

2.8 Right in this area, the trail turns from singletrack to dirt road, then evolves into a more substantial dirt road. Continue climbing up this road.

4.9 Look for the Swede Ridge shelter down to the left of the road if you want to take a break. From the road right above the shelter, you'll take the Swede Ridge Trail, the first trail off to the right. This trail will continue to climb, with a few steeper pitches to keep your legs pumping.

6.9 At the intersection with the Swampy Lakes Trail, turn right.

7.3 Turn right onto South Fork Trail. You'll see a large sign about the Bend Watershed. It's okay; you are on the right trail. Prepare for a fun downhill, but note that this is a two-way trail, so watch for uphill riders.

9.0 Cross the creek here. Mosquitoes can be aggressive in this zone—I once got a flat here and it was challenging, fending off the mozzies while trying to change the flat. A trail takes off to the left to Bridge Creek (no bikes), so stay right on South Fork Trail. From here, the trail follows the creek, with some ups and downs.

10.3 At the intersection with Tumalo Creek Trail, stay right. *Option: To check out Tumalo Falls, turn left for a mile-long out-and-back diversion to the falls.*

12.0 Stay straight on the main trail to avoid going through Skyliners Lodge property.

12.6 Turn left on the short trail that takes you back to Skyliners Sno-Park.

13.3 Return to Skyliners Sno-Park.

OPTIONS

If you are looking for more riding, head to Tumalo Falls to access North Fork Trail. From here, you can ride the North Fork–Farewell loop (see Route 17) or choose from other trails in the high alpine country.

17 NORTH FORK AND FAREWELL

LOOP

Trail Type: 100% singletrack
Distance: 16.6 miles
Elevation Gain/Loss: 1910/1910 feet
High Point: 6262 feet
Ride Time: 2–4 hours
Technical Difficulty: Advanced
Fitness Intensity: Strenuous

Season: July–October
Map: Adventure Maps, Bend, Oregon Trail Map
GPS: 44.0315° N, -121.5150° W
Land Manager: Deschutes National Forest

Farewell Trail offers killer views from the ridge. (Photo: Chris Kratsch)

OVERVIEW

If you are looking for a ride that includes gushing waterfalls, dark forests, and wildflowers, along with some technical riding, this is your ticket. Starting with the ninety-eight-foot-high Tumalo Falls, this ride takes you along North Fork Tumalo Creek past several other waterfalls and through deep hemlock and fir trees. Upon reaching wildflower-laden Happy Valley, the route then takes a short portion of Mrazek Trail to Farewell Trail. The downhill portion of Farewell Trail is a narrow downhill (narrower than most trails in the Bend area) peppered with loose scree sections, steep sidehills, and challenging switchbacks.

The North Fork Trail is a very popular trail for hikers and trail runners, so be prepared to practice your Trail Love. The North Fork Trail is also an uphill-only route for mountain bikers, so there is no downhill riding on this first section. Once you climb up North Fork, you are committed to coming down another way. Because this is a fairly high-elevation ride, there will likely be snow and downed trees on the trails until mid- to late July, so check around and make sure it is clear.

GETTING THERE

From the intersection of NE 3rd Street and NE Greenwood Avenue in Bend, take Greenwood Avenue west. In 1.5 miles, at the roundabout, turn left to head south on NW 14th Street. In 0.4 mile, at the "flaming chicken" round-about, turn right onto Galveston Avenue and head west on what will become Skyliners Road. In 9.7 miles, you'll reach Skyliners Sno-Park on the left. Please watch your speed while driving out here, as this is a quiet neighborhood with a lot of kids and dogs.

MILEAGE LOG

0.0 From Skyliners Sno-Park, take the Tumalo Creek Trail, which starts just to the right of the kiosk and the outhouse.

0.5 Continue through the green gate.

0.6 Cross the creek on a wooden bridge.

0.7 At the intersection of Tumalo Creek Trail and Tumalo Ridge Trail, turn right to stay on Tumalo Creek Trail. *Caution: Tumalo Creek Trail is well loved by mountain bikers, hikers, trail runners, and dog walkers. This*

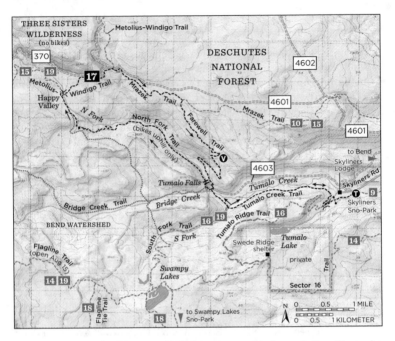

is a fast trail, with several blind corners and tall vegetation. Please be careful and use a bell if you have one.

3.0 At the intersection with South Fork Trail, stay to the right to continue along Tumalo Creek.

3.5 At the Tumalo Falls parking lot, take the steep North Fork Trail up to the falls overlook. Check it out, then hop back on the North Fork Trail to climb, steeply at times, for the next few miles. There are tons of waterfalls along this section!

5.7 Cross the creek on a log bridge.

7.1 You'll encounter a series of logs and bridges through a swampy area. To help protect the riparian zone, use them—even if you have to walk your bike.

7.3 At Happy Valley, take the bridge to the right to cross the creek. You are now on Metolius–Windigo Trail.

8.4 At this big intersection of FR 370 and FR 4601, look for Mrazek Trail and head east on Mrazek.

9.9 Turn right onto Farewell Trail. *Option: Arrange a shuttle and, instead of coming down Farewell Trail, ride Mrazek Trail all the way back to Shevlin Park in Bend (see Route 10).*

11.5 If you want to stop for photos, there are some nice views here. Expect some fun, rocky tread along this section.

13.1 After the steep, tight switchbacks, you'll pop out at the bottom onto FR 4603. Turn right onto the road, toward the falls, then take a left onto Tumalo Creek Trail.

13.6 Stay left on Tumalo Creek Trail.

15.9 Stay straight on the main trails to avoid going through Skyliners Lodge property.

16.0 Turn left to take the short trail back to Skyliners Sno-Park.

16.6 Finish the ride at Skyliners Sno-Park.

18 SWAMPY LAKES AND VISTA BUTTE

LOOP

Trail Type: 100% singletrack
Distance: 8.1 miles
Elevation Gain/Loss: 1060/1060 feet
High Point: 6613 feet
Ride Time: 1–1.5 hours
Technical Difficulty: Intermediate
Fitness Intensity: Moderate

Season: June–October
Map: Adventure Maps, Bend, Oregon Trail Map
GPS: 43.9898° N, -121.5678° W
Land Manager: Deschutes National Forest

OVERVIEW

This is a fairly quick ride that includes a short climb to the summit of Vista Butte. It is a nice early morning jaunt in the heat of midsummer, but it can get dry and dusty, so try to hit it after a bit of rain.

The Swampy Lakes area is laced with a myriad of summertime singletrack and wintertime ski trails. The place is covered in ski trail intersections and signs, so it can get confusing at times to know where you are. Fortunately, all of the signs can get you back to the parking area.

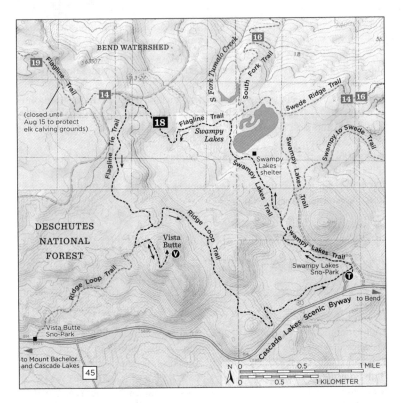

From this area, you can access a lot of good stuff, so check out a map and see what you can link up.

GETTING THERE

From the intersection of NE 3rd Street and NE Greenwood Avenue in Bend, take Greenwood Avenue west. In 1.5 miles, at the roundabout, turn left to head south on NW 14th Street. At the "flaming chicken" roundabout, stay straight to continue on NW 14th Street, which eventually becomes Cascade Lakes Scenic Byway. At 15.5 miles, turn right into Swampy Lakes Sno-Park.

MILEAGE LOG

0.0 From the Swampy Lakes trailhead, head straight on the main Swampy Lakes Trail. Don't take the first trail to your left. You'll be coming back down that trail at the end.

0.1 Take the second trail to the left, the Swampy Lakes Trail.

0.8 The eastern branch of the Swampy Lakes Trail takes off to the right. Stay straight here.

1.7 The Swampy Lakes shelter is to your right.

2.0 Turn left at Flagline Trail.

3.1 Turn left at Flagline Tie Trail. *Note: The upper reach of Flagline Trail (if you were to continue straight here) is closed until August 15 to protect elk calving habitat. Please respect this closure. Do it for the baby elk.*

4.3 At this intersection of Flagline Tie and Ridge Loop Trail, you can make a short climb up to Vista Butte. Turn right to opt in for Vista Butte. I recommend it. *Option: If you don't want to ride up Vista Butte, turn left on Ridge Loop Trail to take you back to Swampy Lakes Sno-Park.*

4.6 Turn left here to continue up to Vista Butte. The trail gets considerably steeper here and the last little bit up to the top will be loose, red cinder rocks.

Early morning on Vista Butte

5.1 You're at the top of Vista Butte. Grab a seat on a makeshift bench to chill out and check out the 360-degree view, then turn around and go back down the way you came.

5.6 Turn right onto Ridge Loop Trail.

5.9 At the intersection with Flagline Tie, stay straight on Ridge Loop Trail. This is a fun little descent back down to Swampy Lakes Sno-Park.

8.1 Return to the Swampy Lakes Sno-Park parking lot.

OPTIONS

After the end of the trail closure on August 15, you can ride up and back on Flagline Trail to add more miles to this ride.

19 NORTH FORK, METOLIUS–WINDIGO, AND SOUTH FORK

LOOP

Trail Type: 100% singletrack
Distance: 24.5 miles
Elevation Gain/Loss: 3050/3050 feet
High Point: 6980 feet
Ride Time: 4–6 hours
Technical Difficulty: Advanced
Fitness Intensity: Very strenuous

Season: August 15–October
Map: Adventure Maps, Bend, Oregon Trail Map
GPS: 44.0315° N, -121.5150° W
Land Manager: Deschutes National Forest

OVERVIEW

Every time I ride this fantastic loop, I think about the first time I ever rode it. It was 1997 and I was new to Bend, and I was also fairly new to mountain biking and had just started riding with clipless pedals. Along with my husband and a good friend, John Gonter, I embarked on this ride looking for a good adventure, because at the time, 25 miles and 3000 feet of climbing was epic considering we had heavy steel hardtail bikes to push around. For food, we brought peanut butter and jelly sandwiches and a stove with instant soup

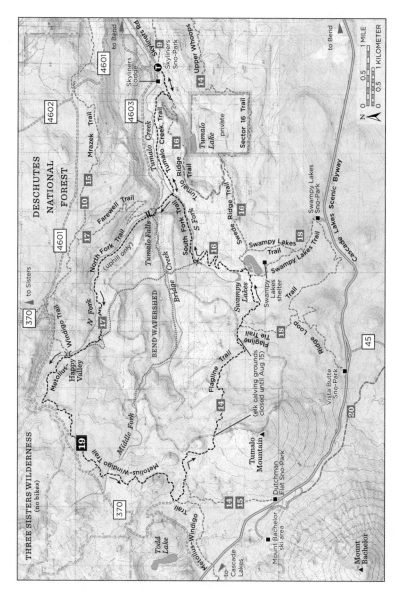

packets—I don't know what we were thinking! John fired up the stove about midway along the ride in a beautiful alpine meadow and made us hot soup. Ever since then, I try to get this ride in every summer.

Though this loop is not considered "epic" by today's standards, it is a tough ride with plenty of climbing and some technical spots. It follows the perimeter of the Bend Watershed, up North Fork Trail with its numerous waterfalls to Metolius–Windigo Trail, which winds through the high country, to then head back via Flagline and South Fork trails. South Fork Trail is a rough-and-tumble downhill with root drops, water bars, and challenging tread.

Keep in mind that Flagline Trail is completely closed until August 15 every year to protect elk and their calves. Volunteer trail crews try to clear the trail of downed trees on August 15; but if there is a lot of downfall, it can take several days to clear. It's also a very high-elevation ride that doesn't clear of snow until about then, or even later, so it is best ridden after late August. This is a remote ride, so be prepared to be self-sufficient in the backcountry.

GETTING THERE

From the intersection of NE 3rd Street and NE Greenwood Avenue in Bend, take Greenwood Avenue west. In 1.5 miles, at the roundabout, turn left to head south on NW 14th Street. In 0.4 mile, at the "flaming chicken" roundabout, turn right onto Galveston Avenue and head west on what will become Skyliners Road. In 9.7 miles, you'll reach Skyliners Sno-Park on the left. Please watch your speed while driving out here, as this is a quiet neighborhood with a lot of kids and dogs.

MILEAGE LOG

0.0   From Skyliners Sno-Park, take Tumalo Creek Trail, just to the right of the outhouse.

0.7   After crossing the creek, take Tumalo Creek Trail to the right.

3.0   After crossing the creek, turn right again. South Fork Trail, which you will come down later in the ride, is to your left at this intersection.

3.5   At the Tumalo Falls parking lot, take the trail up to the falls and beyond. This is the North Fork Trail and you will climb alongside the creek, passing several waterfalls along the way. This is an uphill-only trail for bikes, and you'll likely see a few hikers or trail runners.

7.3   At Happy Valley, stay straight on Metolius–Windigo Trail. This is a very nice section of trail that rolls through a mix of forest and open meadows, with some creek crossings and steep climbs.

Crossing North Fork Tumalo Creek on the North Fork Trail (Photo: Chris Kratsch)

10.5 Stay straight on Metolius–Windigo Trail. The trail to the right goes to FR 370 if you need an emergency bailout point.

12.8 Turn left at Flagline Trail.

13.5 Stay straight on Flagline Trail and get ready to climb a bit partway up the side of Tumalo Mountain.

17.4 At the intersection with Flagline Tie Trail, stay straight on Flagline. You are now entering the Swampy Lakes Nordic ski area.

18.5 Stay left here onto the Swampy Lakes Trail.

18.6 Turn left onto South Fork Trail. You'll see a large sign about the Bend Watershed. It's okay; you are on the right trail. Prepare for a rowdy and fun downhill down South Fork.

21.6 At the intersection of South Fork Trail and Tumalo Creek Trail, turn right onto Tumalo Creek Trail. This is a popular trail that has some fast, blind corners and is heavily used for hiking and running. Be careful and courteous.

23.8 After a short uphill, turn left. The trail to the right is Tumalo Ridge Trail.

24.5 End the ride at Skyliners Sno-Park.

OPTIONS

If you're into a longer, epic, 50-mile ride, try starting in Bend or at Phil's trailhead so you can earn an extra serving at the pub afterward.

20 RIDE AROUND MOUNT BACHELOR

LOOP

Trail Type: 70% singletrack, 30% dirt road
Distance: 31.2 miles
Elevation Gain/Loss: 2920/2920 feet
High Point: 6450 feet
Ride Time: 4–6 hours
Technical Difficulty: Advanced–expert

Fitness Intensity: Very strenuous
Season: August–October
Map: Adventure Maps, Bend, Oregon Trail Map
GPS: 43.9141° N, -121.7675° W
Land Manager: Deschutes National Forest

OVERVIEW

The "ride around Bachee" is a rite of passage of sorts in the central Oregon mountain biking tribe. Rumor has it that, back in the day, the first pioneering mountain bikers put on a race around the mountain that included riding portions of alpine ski get-back trails that traverse the mountain. I imagine that was a very long ride on the heavy, rigid bikes of that time.

This ride has a little bit of everything. The first climb, from Lava Lake heading east, is a doozy, with steep sections of loose lava rock. The downhills, especially from Mount Bachelor ski area on the Metolius–Windigo Trail, are worth the effort, though. It's a solid ride, so plan for a full day.

There are many ways to do this ride, starting in different locations. My write-up below reflects what I believe to be the "best" way to do it. Everyone has his or her own opinion of course, but this way gets you the longest downhill from Sparks Lake back to Lava Lake. I've also shaped this route to be all dirt and no pavement. Here's the caveat—the dirt road portion from the intersection of Forest Road 45 and Cascade Lakes Scenic Byway is quite brutal. It is a very loose, sandy uphill dirt road with sections of unrideable "baby heads." Keep an eye out for motorized vehicles, such as ATVs and motorcycles, along this stretch. If you opt for riding pavement, this would be a good place to make that choice. Or, if you are dead set on riding all dirt, go for it.

Routefinding is challenging on this ride, particularly when entering and leaving Edison Butte Sno-Park and near the West Village Lodge at Mount

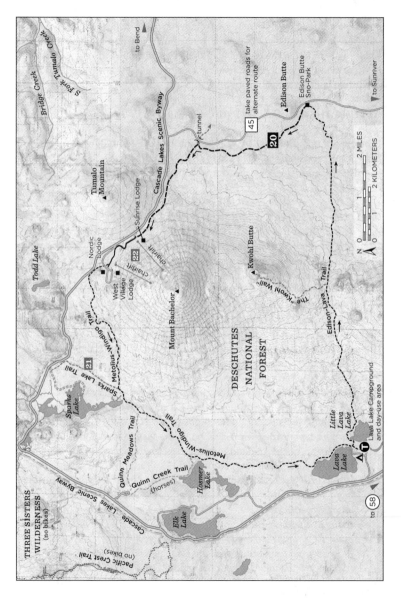

Bachelor ski area. I've written my best description of how to find the trails, but there are several ways to do it, so be patient if you don't find the trail right away. I've also noted the technical difficulty as advanced to expert. Most of it is fairly technical with some "expert" sections along the way—places where you might get off and walk your bike.

GETTING THERE

From Bend, take Century Drive (Cascade Lakes Scenic Byway) all the way past Mount Bachelor to Lava Lake, about 38 miles from Bend. Park at the day-use area near the boat ramp and campground at Lava Lake.

MILEAGE LOG

0.0 From the Lava Lake boat ramp parking lot, take the trail east.

0.1 Turn right at this first trail junction to head toward Little Lava Lake.

1.3 Stay straight/left on the Edison–Lava Trail. Here you will start climbing up some challenging terrain, with sharp, loose lava rock baby heads.

4.8 You are more or less at the top of this climb. Yay! *Option: The ATV/ motorcycle road up to the left ascends Kwohl Butte, also known as the "Kwohl Wall." It's an 800-foot climb in 2.1 miles—brutal. If you go up the wall, just turn around and come back down the same trail.*

7.7 You'll start seeing other wide trails in this area. These are the Edison Butte Sno-Park cross-country ski trails. Stay on the main Edison–Lava Trail to go to Edison Butte Sno-Park.

10.4 You've reached Edison Butte Sno-Park. You have two choices here. If you need a break and want to hit the pavement, you can go out to FR 45 and turn left (north) up toward Cascade Lakes Scenic Byway, then turn left (west) to continue on pavement to Mount Bachelor ski area. Or if you want to stay on dirt the whole way, continue through to the north end of the parking lot and take the dirt road that leaves from there. This road will roughly parallel FR 45.

14.3 When you get to the tunnel that goes under the highway, turn left onto this much-improved and well-graveled dirt road that parallels Cascade Lakes Scenic Byway. *Option: If you are over it and really want pavement now, take Cascade Lakes Scenic Byway to Mount Bachelor ski area.*

17.2 Ride past Sunrise Lodge at Mount Bachelor ski area. Keep going on this road past the Junior Race Center and on toward West Village Lodge.

Flying over rocks on the Edison–Lava Trail

18.7 At the main West Village Lodge, you'll need to get on the Metolius–Windigo Trail. The easiest way to find it is to start at the Nordic Lodge, then ride down the "common corridor" toward the highway. Just before the highway, the trail crosses the common corridor. This section of trail is a blast, but watch for loose pumice corners and surprise lava rocks.

22.8 At the intersection with Sparks Lake Trail, stay left on Metolius–Windigo.

23.8 Quinn Meadows Trail takes off to the right. Stay straight on Metolius–Windigo.

25.8 The Quinn Creek Trail to Hosmer Lake takes off to the right. Stay on Metolius–Windigo Trail. *Caution: Watch for equestrians from here on. This area is popular with horseback riders.*

29.6 You've reached the north end of Lava Lake. Continue on the same trail.

31.1 At the Edison–Lava Trail intersection, stay right. You are almost done.

31.2 Return to the Lava Lake parking lot. They have candy bars in the little store at Lava Lake if you need one. I usually do after this ride!

21 LAVA LAKE TO SPARKS LAKE

OUT-AND-BACK

Trail Type: 90% singletrack, 10% dirt road
Distance: 25.6 miles
Elevation Gain/Loss: 1550/1550 feet
High Point: 5593 feet
Ride Time: 1–4 hours
Technical Difficulty: Advanced

Fitness Intensity: Strenuous
Season: July–October
Map: Adventure Maps, Bend, Oregon Trail Map
GPS: 43.9141° N, -121.7675° W
Land Manager: Deschutes National Forest

OVERVIEW

If you find yourself camping up at the high lakes in the summer, this ride will give you a sampling of three lakes—Lava, Hosmer, and Sparks. You'll also get some very nice views of the backside of Mount Bachelor. The ride, from Lava Lake to Sparks Lake, utilizes a good portion of the Metolius–Windigo Trail as well as the Sparks Lake Trail.

This is a high-elevation ride, so midsummer to late summer is best, after the trail has been cleared of downed trees. This ride is also best done after some rain as it can be loose and "pummie" (made up of loose pumice rock) when it is really dry out. Parts of this trail are used by equestrians, so be aware and courteous. It is possible to do this ride as a shuttle from Sparks Lake down to Lava Lake if you don't want to put in the work to climb up the trail.

GETTING THERE

From Bend, take Century Drive (Cascade Lakes Scenic Byway) all the way past Mount Bachelor to Lava Lake, about 38 miles from Bend. Park at the day-use area near the boat ramp and campground at Lava Lake.

MILEAGE LOG

0.0 From the Lava Lake day-use area parking lot, take the short trail east and turn left on the Metolius–Windigo Trail to ride north.

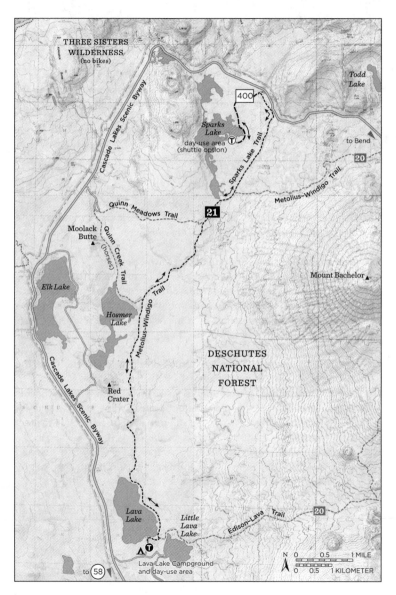

THREE SISTERS
WILDERNESS
(no bikes)

Todd
Lake

Cascade Lakes Scenic Byway

400

Sparks
Lake

day-use area
(shuttle option)

Sparks Lake Trail

to Bend

20

Metolius–Windigo Trail

Quinn Meadows Trail

21

Moolack
Butte

Quinn Creek Trail

(horses)

Elk Lake

Hosmer
Lake

Metolius–Windigo Trail

Mount Bachelor

DESCHUTES

NATIONAL

FOREST

Red
Crater

Cascade Lakes Scenic Byway

Lava
Lake

Little
Lava
Lake

Edison–Lava Trail

20

N   0   0.5   1 MILE

0   0.5   1 KILOMETER

to 58

Lava Lake Campground
and day-use area

Navigating lava rock near Lava Lake (Photo: Chris Kratsch)

1.5 You are now at the very north end of Lava Lake.

5.3 At the intersection with Quinn Creek Trail, turn right to stay on the Metolius–Windigo Trail. From here, you might see some horseback riders on the trail, so keep your eyes and ears open. The trail also gets a bit steeper and more technical for the next few miles.

7.3 Quinn Meadows Trail takes off to the left. Stay straight on Metolius–Windigo.

8.3 Here, the Metolius–Windigo Trail turns east at the intersection with the Sparks Lake Trail. Turn left on Sparks Lake Trail.

11.3 At the intersection of the Sparks Lake Trail, Cascade Lakes Scenic Byway, and FR 400, you have the option (recommended) to take FR 400 south to Sparks Lake. Or you can turn around on the trail to head back the way you came.

12.8 At the end of FR 400, you'll be at the Sparks Lake day-use area and boat launch. This is a great spot to have some lunch and hang out by the lake. When you're ready, head back down FR 400 to the trail.

14.3 Get on the Sparks Lake Trail.

17.3 At the intersection with the Metolius–Windigo Trail, turn right. Keep an eye out for equestrians.

20.3 Stay straight on Metolius–Windigo where Quinn Creek Trail takes off to the right.

25.6 Return to the Lava Lake parking area where you started the ride.

22 MOUNT BACHELOR BIKE PARK

NETWORK

Trail Type: 100% singletrack and/or wide flow trail
Distance: Up to 15 miles
Elevation Gain/Loss: 0/1350 feet
High Point: 7775 feet
Ride Time: From open to close, if desired!
Technical Difficulty: Intermediate–expert

Fitness Intensity: Easy–strenuous
Season: July–September
Map: Mount Bachelor Bike Park trail map
GPS: 43.9918° N, -121.6934° W
Land Managers: Deschutes National Forest; Mount Bachelor ski area
Permit: Mount Bachelor Bike Park chairlift ticket

OVERVIEW

In 2013, after many years of community input and deliberation, Mount Bachelor ski area finally invested in summertime recreation with their lift-accessed downhill mountain biking park. This is a big deal for central Oregon, as the park provides more significant elevation loss than any other trail system east of the Cascades. Like downhill skiing, the trails are labeled from "green circle" to "double black diamond" and are a mix of machine-built "flow trails" and narrower hand-built trails, providing something for everyone.

Two lifts take you to the top of the trails, and all of the trails are one-way, downhill-only trails. The Pine Marten lift accesses the intermediate through very expert trails and the Sunshine lift accesses the shorter beginner trails. There is also a skills park at the bottom of the lifts—great for riders of all ages. In 2016, the summer mountain biking season was open from July 1 until September 5, but this may vary depending on the weather. In the summer, the eatery Scapolos at Pine Marten Lodge is open for lunches every day and for "Sunset Dinners" on Fridays, Saturdays, and Sundays. There is an espresso bar that is open every day as well.

Mount Bachelor requires the following items to ride the trails: a lift ticket, a helmet, closed-toe shoes, and a bike with functioning front and rear brakes. Because these really are downhill trails, they strongly recommend

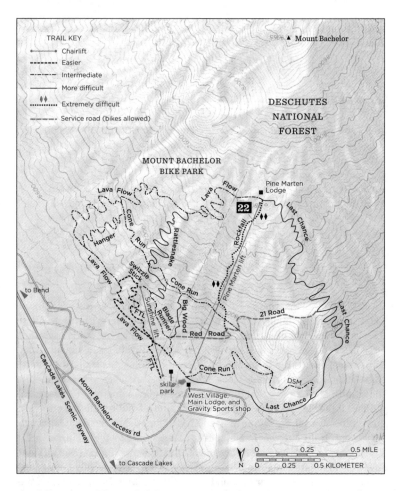

the following: a bike with full suspension (at least five inches of travel) and disc brakes, a full-face helmet, and armor/padding and gloves.

The Gravity Sports shop, located in the West Village, rents and sells downhill-specific mountain bikes, as well as helmets, pads, clothing, and supplies. They also have a repair shop to service your bike. Visit the

Many of the Mount Bachelor Bike Park trails are flow trails with bermed corners and open sight lines.

Mount Bachelor website to get a full map and description of the bike park: www.mtbachelor.com.

Although these are all "downhill routes," I've listed the technical difficulty as intermediate to expert as there is a wide range of skills needed for different trails. Fitness intensity is easy to strenuous—if you ride all day, you'll get pretty tired!

GETTING THERE

From the intersection of NE 3rd Street and NE Greenwood Avenue in Bend, take Greenwood Avenue west. In 1.5 miles, at the roundabout, turn left to head south on NW 14th Street, which eventually turns into Cascade Lakes

Follow this suggestion at Mount Bachelor Bike Park!

Scenic Byway. At 20.9 miles, stay left to reach the Mount Bachelor West Village and main lodge. You'll purchase your lift ticket here.

MILEAGE LOG

Included here are mileages, slopes, and other features for the trails. The slopes listed are averages for the entire trail, so be prepared for sections that are steeper or flatter along the way.

Easier "green circle" trails, accessed from the Sunshine lift:

First Timer Line (FTL): 0.7 mile and 7% slope. This is the easiest trail with gentle dips, rolls, and turns.

Swizzle Stick: 0.1 mile and 11% slope. Connects Lava Flow to FTL.

Lava Flow, lower portion: 0.8 mile and 6% slope. Lower Lava is the widest flow trail on the mountain and a good practice run for those new to downhill mountain biking.

Intermediate "blue square" trails, accessed from the Sunshine lift and Pine Marten lift:

Lava Flow, upper portion: 3.9 miles and 7% slope. This flow trail begins in lava rock, then winds through mountain hemlock forest, with jumps, turns, berms, and rollers.

Hanger: 0.6 mile and 9% slope. Take this trail for a narrower alternative to the middle portion of Lava Flow.

Blade Runner: 0.4 mile, 11% slope. This is a narrower alternative to the FTL or Lava Flow that will take you to the bottom of the lift.

Cone Run: 2.0 miles and 6% slope. Traversing the mountain, then winding around the cinder cone, this trail also includes numerous wooden features and jumps.

DSM: 0.4 mile and 7% slope. This trail is a machine-built trail with rollers, jumps, dips, and fast corners.

More difficult and extremely difficult "black diamond and double black diamond" trails, accessed from the Pine Marten lift:

Rattlesnake: 1.2 miles and 12% slope. One of the first trails built, this route is a technical singletrack that crosses a half-pipe.

Big Wood: 0.3 mile and 21% slope. This trail has a few challenging wood features, steeper sections, and the option to take a big drop at the end.

Last Chance: 3.8 miles and 7% slope. Last Chance is the most remote trail on the mountain; don't be fooled by the average slope, as there are very steep sections.

Rockfall: 0.8 mile and 20% gradient. As the name suggests, this is the steepest, hardest trail at the park, with a "double black diamond" label.

WALDO LAKE

If there were a Land o' Lakes region in Oregon, the southern end of the Cascades high lakes and the Waldo Lake area might be it. Surrounding these blue lakes are steep hillsides covered in mountain hemlock and alpine fir forests with yummy singletrack trails that are prime from midsummer to late summer and fall. I've included a few lake rides, as well as some rides that have you climbing up old volcanic peaks, then screaming back down.

From Bend, you can access this area either by taking Cascade Lakes Scenic Byway all the way around Mount Bachelor, or by taking US Highway 97 to Oregon Route 58 to Willamette Pass. Either way, Waldo Lake is about a one-and-a-half-hour drive from Bend. There isn't much in the way of amenities near these rides, but I've noted some services, such as food and lodging (for more, see Resources, Visit Central Oregon). There are great camping options in the area, mostly in Forest Service campgrounds near the lakes.

Other than the steep climbs and technical trails, the main challenge for riding is mosquitoes. They can be ferocious, so waiting until later in the summer, when the weather dries out and the populations die down, is a good idea. Otherwise, bring the DEET!

23 WALDO LAKE TRAIL

LOOP

Trail Type: 100% singletrack
Distance: 20.2 miles
Elevation Gain/Loss: 1390/1390 feet

High Point: 5765 feet
Ride Time: 3–5 hours
Technical Difficulty: Advanced

Opposite: *There are plenty of big trees and buffed-out trails in the Waldo Lake area.* (Photo: Chris Kratsch)

Fitness Intensity: Strenuous
Season: July–October
Map: Adventure Maps, Bend, Oregon Trail Map
GPS: 43.7612° N, -122.0045° W

Land Manager: Willamette National Forest
Permit: NW Forest Pass (annual or day pass)

OVERVIEW

Waldo Lake is a true Oregon Cascades gem. As one of the purest lakes in the world, it is crystal clear and very cold—pure snowmelt. The best times to ride here are from late August through early October, when the mosquitoes have subsided and the trail is cleared and free of snow and downed trees.

Don't be fooled by the "lake ride" descriptor. This is a rugged and remote ride; and for only 20 miles of singletrack, you'll get your money's worth. The trail is technical, twisty, rooty, rocky, at times fast, then slow, and constantly up or down. The entire northern, western, and southern parts of the trail are bordered by the Waldo Lake Wilderness, where bikes are prohibited, so please respect this rule. Also, be prepared with adequate food, water, and first-aid and mechanical supplies. It's a long way to civilization when you are on the other side of the lake, and there are no commercial facilities at the lake.

I prefer to start this ride at North Waldo, the northeast end of the lake, and ride counterclockwise. This way, you end the ride on a cruiser section of trail back to North Waldo. But of course, you can mix it up on this loop ride. Waldo Lake is also a good starting point for some exceptional rides in these parts: Lemish and Charlton lakes (Route 24), the Twins (Route 26), Mount Ray and Fuji Mountain (Route 28), and more.

By the way, the Waldo Lake Trail is officially named the Jim Weaver Trail, after a former Oregon congressman, so you will likely see that signage at some point. All day-use areas at Waldo Lake, including North Waldo, require a Northwest Forest Pass. All campgrounds at Waldo Lake also require a camping fee.

GETTING THERE

From Bend, take US Highway 97 South until you reach the Crescent Cutoff Road (County Road 61) in the town of Crescent (there is a Shell gas station

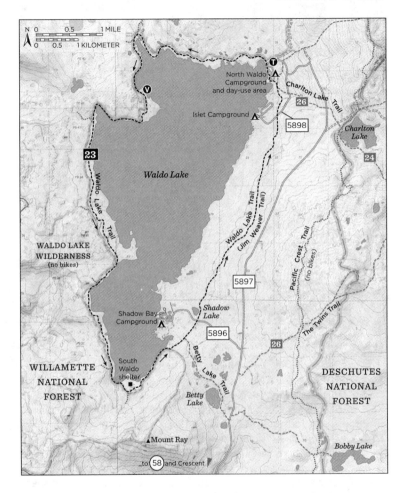

on the corner). Turn right here. In another 24 miles, turn right onto Oregon Route 58. About 3 miles past the Willamette Pass ski area, turn right on paved Forest Road 5897. Follow this road 13 miles until you reach the North Waldo day-use area.

The Waldo Lake route starts in an old burn. (Photo: Heidi Faller)

MILEAGE LOG

0.0 From the North Waldo day-use area, near North Waldo Campground, head west on the Waldo Lake Trail, signed as the Jim Weaver Trail.

0.5 You'll enter a large burned area, legacy of a forest fire that scorched the whole north side of the lake in 1996.

2.5 As you ride back into the dark forest and among the big trees, you'll pass through some swampy areas. Stay on the constructed wood boardwalks and log bridges so you don't disturb the riparian ecology.

4.6 Traverse a big scree slope to an awesome vantage point and snack spot. For the next 8 miles, you'll contour the west bank of the lake, where you'll find a string of good swimming holes. All trails that go off to the right enter the Waldo Lake Wilderness and are closed to bikes. You may come across hikers and backpackers along this section. The trail is literally up and down, up and down—with some very technical, but short, descents.

12.4 When you reach the South Waldo shelter you'll know you are at the south end of the lake. The upcoming section, the east side of the lake, is smoother and faster, but still has a lot of rolling hills.

14.4 The Betty Lake Trail takes off to the right; stay straight on the Waldo Lake Trail. *Option: This is a beautiful trail to Betty Lake, about 3 miles roundtrip, if you are looking for more riding. From Betty Lake, you can also ride toward the Twins (Route 26).*

14.7 Cross FR 5896 (access for Shadow Bay Campground) and continue on the trail.

17.1 You're at the highest point of the ride!

19.1 Cross FR 5898 (the road that leads to Islet Campground), and stay straight on the trail.

20.2 Return to North Waldo Campground and the parking area.

24 LEMISH AND CHARLTON LAKES

LOOP

Trail Type: 80% singletrack, 20% dirt road
Distance: 18 miles
Elevation Gain/Loss: 1710/1710 feet
High Point: 5910 feet
Ride Time: 3–4 hours
Technical Difficulty: Advanced

Fitness Intensity: Strenuous
Season: August–October
Map: Adventure Maps, Bend, Oregon Trail Map
GPS: 43.8000° N, -121.8636° W
Land Manager: Deschutes National Forest

OVERVIEW

This is one of my favorite high lakes rides to do with a group of friends. The trail is just technical and interesting enough to keep you on your toes, with plenty of steep pitches and rooty sections. It also goes through some fabulous fir forests on the first half of the loop. This ride, like many other high lakes rides, is best done later in the summer or early in the fall when the mosquitoes have subsided. It's also a common trail for lots of blowdown: check on trail conditions before you go, so you won't be hiking your bike over tons of trees.

Charlton Lake and Charlton Lake Trail (Photo: Chris Kratsch)

I like to start this ride at Little Cultus Lake. This way, you get a bit of a warm-up on a dirt road and you get to end the ride with a swim in Little Cultus.

GETTING THERE

From Bend, take Century Drive (Cascade Lakes Scenic Byway) and follow it all the way past Mount Bachelor, Sparks Lake, Elk Lake, and Lava and Little Lava lakes. At about 43 miles, turn right onto Forest Road 4635 to go to Cultus Lake. In 0.8 mile, before you get to Cultus Lake, turn left onto FR 4630. In 2.5 miles, park at Little Cultus Lake, just west of the campground.

MILEAGE LOG

0.0 Start at the Little Cultus Lake parking area. Take FR 4636 west.

2.0 Get on the Charlton Lake Trail at the Lemish Lake trailhead.

2.8 At Lemish Lake, turn right on the trail to Charlton Lake. The trail from here to Charlton is "busy," with plenty of roots, some rocks, and some very steep, but usually short, climbs.

5.5 At the intersection with Lily Lake Trail, stay straight/left on the Charlton Lake Trail.

5.7 Clover Meadow Trail will take off to the left. *Option: For a much shorter loop, take this trail to connect over to the east side of the loop.*

7.6 Cross FR 4290 and descend to Charlton Lake.

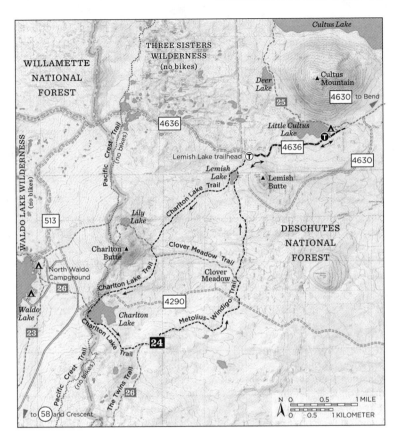

8.0 Check out the nice swimming spot at Charlton Lake. The trail to Waldo Lake also takes off right around here, as well as the Pacific Crest Trail (PCT), where no bikes are allowed.

8.2 The PCT takes off to the right (south). Continue around the south side of Charlton Lake.

9.2 Watch for some really steep and technical downhills as you wrap around the south side of the lake.

10.2 The Twins Trail takes off to the right, but stay straight here. You are now on a portion of the Metolius–Windigo Trail, which you will take back to Lemish Lake. This side of the loop is a fair bit easier with smoother tread and less climbing.

12.2 Cross FR 4290 and stay straight on Metolius–Windigo Trail.

12.7 Clover Meadow Trail takes off to the left. Stay straight on Metolius–Windigo Trail.

15.8 You are now back at Lemish Lake, so turn right here to descend to the Lemish Lake trailhead.

16.1 At the Lemish Lake trailhead, take FR 4636 back to Little Cultus Lake, where you parked your car.

18.0 End the ride at Little Cultus Lake.

OPTIONS

Combine this ride and Waldo Lake (see Route 23) for a really swell, long (about 40 miles), and challenging day of mountain biking.

25 CULTUS LAKE

LOOP

Trail Type: 70% singletrack, 20% dirt road, 10% pavement
Distance: 11.7 miles
Elevation Gain/Loss: 730/730 feet
High Point: 4929 feet
Ride Time: 1–2 hours
Technical Difficulty: Beginner

Fitness Intensity: Moderate
Season: July–October
Map: Adventure Maps, Bend, Oregon Trail Map
GPS: 43.8325° N, -121.8321° W
Land Manager: Deschutes National Forest

OVERVIEW

If you are camping up at the high lakes anywhere along Cascade Lakes Scenic Byway, the Cultus Lake loop is a nice little spin for a beginner rider. As with all lake loops, a requisite jump in the water is the perfect way to end the ride. Cultus Lake is one of the many popular lakes for camping, boating, and fishing; and the Cultus Lake Resort is famous for its tasty milkshakes and is a nice place to hang out to watch the sunset.

You can't help but smile on these trails. (Photo: Heidi Faller)

Although the trail may be clear of snow by June, know that this is an area that can have a lot of trees downed from winter storms. Even more important, like at many of the high lakes, the mosquitoes can be seriously ferocious, so I recommend riding this later in the summer or early in the fall.

GETTING THERE

From Bend, take Century Drive (Cascade Lakes Scenic Byway) and follow it all the way past Mount Bachelor, Sparks Lake, Elk Lake, and Lava and Little

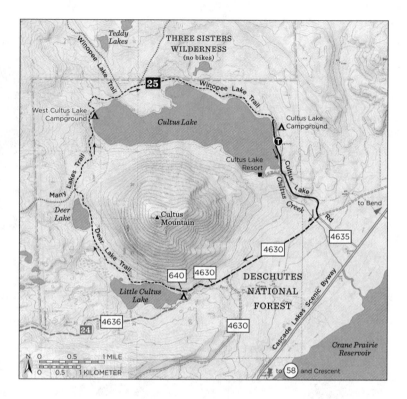

Lava lakes. At about 43 miles, turn right onto Cultus Lake Road (Forest Road 4635) and continue straight to Cultus Lake. Go past the turn to Cultus Lake Resort on the left, then park at the first day-use parking area alongside the road just before you get to the main boat ramp and campground.

MILEAGE LOG

0.0   From the day-use area, take FR 4635 southeast, back toward Cascade Lakes Scenic Byway.

1.1   Turn right onto gravel FR 4630. You'll be climbing, so be sure to stay to the right for cars to pass. This can be a heavily traveled road on a summer weekend.

2.8   Stay straight on FR 4630 toward Little Cultus Lake.

3.5 At Little Cultus Lake, turn right at FR 640. You'll see a small camp-ground here on the banks of the lake.

3.8 Look for Deer Lake Trail to the left and take this trail to skirt Little Cultus Lake. You might want to keep your mosquito repellent handy now. The trail will climb gradually to Deer Lake and beyond.

5.8 At the intersection where Many Lakes Trail goes to the left, stay straight/right. This portion of the Many Lakes Trail goes into the Three Sisters Wilderness, where no bikes are allowed. However, you will con-tinue around the lake on what is also named the Many Lakes Trail for this section. From here, you'll descend a bit to Cultus Lake. Watch out for dry, sandy corners in this area.

7.4 You might start to hear music and a party scene as you come up to West Cultus Lake Campground. This is a boat-in-only only camping area; and if you look really thirsty, someone might give you a cold beverage. You just never know!

8.4 From here on, stay to the right at all trail junctions. All the trails that go left go into the wilderness; instead, you'll stay on the main trail (Winopee Lake Trail) along the northern shore of Cultus Lake. The forest gets greener here, which means the skeeters fire up again. Ride fast.

11.2 When you enter Cultus Lake Campground, follow the main road along the lake to get back to your vehicle.

11.7 Return to your car. I recommend the milkshakes at Cultus Lake Resort. They are quite tasty on a warm summer day.

26 THE TWINS

LOOP

Trail Type: 95% singletrack, 5% pavement
Distance: 19 miles
Elevation Gain/Loss: 2680/2680 feet
High Point: 7272 feet
Ride Time: 3–5 hours
Technical Difficulty: Advanced
Fitness Intensity: Strenuous

Season: July–October
Map: Adventure Maps, Bend, Oregon Trail Map
GPS: 43.7612° N, -122.0045° W
Land Managers: Willamette National Forest; Deschutes National Forest

Climb up the Twins and you'll be rewarded with this view.

OVERVIEW

The Twins ride is a fantastic addition if you are camping at Waldo Lake and want to ride more than the lake loop (see Route 23). It features some very steep climbing, some hike-a-bike sections, and portions of the Waldo Lake Trail and Charlton Lake Trail.

This ride can be done in either direction. I prefer to do the loop in a counter-clockwise fashion because I like to get a nice warm-up on the east side of Waldo Lake before grunting up the Twins. However, the other way is just as fun, and you get a steeper, smoother descent off the south side of the Twins. This is a pretty substantial climb, and I've included the full summit in my write-up in case you want to hike your bike up to the top and "pumice surf" back down through the loose cinders. The Twins summit offers up a sublime view of Waldo Lake.

This route crosses the Pacific Crest Trail (PCT), so you might see some hikers and backpackers. Please respect the hiker-only designation on the PCT.

GETTING THERE

From Bend, take US Highway 97 South until you reach the Crescent Cutoff Road (County Road 61) in the town of Crescent (there is a Shell gas station

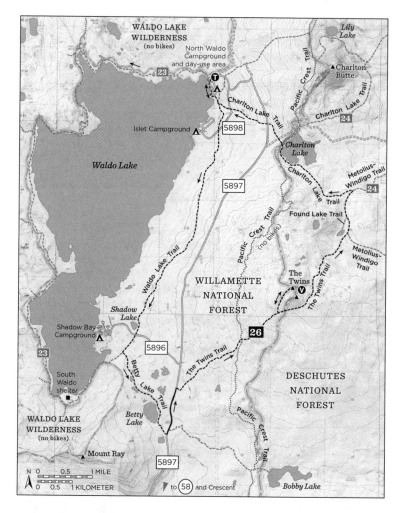

on the corner). Turn right here. In another 24 miles, turn right onto Oregon Route 58. About 3 miles past the Willamette Pass ski area, turn right on paved Forest Road 5897. Follow this road 13 miles until you reach the North Waldo day-use area.

MILEAGE LOG

0.0   Start at North Waldo Campground and day-use area. Ride south on the Waldo Lake Trail, also called the Jim Weaver Trail, on the east side of the lake.

0.5   At the intersection with the Charlton Lake Trail, stay straight to continue on the Waldo Lake Trail.

1.1   Go straight across FR 5898 (the road that leads to Islet Campground). From here, the trail is smooth, wide, and rolling as you head south toward Shadow Bay.

5.4   Cross FR 5896 (the road that leads to Shadow Bay Campground) and continue on the Waldo Lake Trail.

5.7   Take the steep left onto the Betty Lake Trail. You might need to get a running start.

6.8   Pass pretty Betty Lake, to your right.

7.4   Turn left at paved FR 5897 and head north.

8.5   Look for The Twins Trail on the right. (The sign says "Twin Peaks.") Get ready to climb. It starts off mellow but gets seriously steep pretty quick.

10.1   Cross the PCT (no bikes allowed), and continue on The Twins Trail.

10.8   To reach the summit of the Twins, turn left at this intersection. It is very steep, with sections of hiking your bike on loose cinders, but it is worth the view. The Twins is really two peaks and it is possible to ride both of them, with some hiking. When you are done, go back down the way you came.

11.8   Back at the main Twins Trail, turn left to continue around the southeast side of the peaks.

12.3   After a 0.5-mile climb, the downhill begins—finally!—on narrow, bumpy, twisty singletrack through some pumice slopes and fields and forest.

14.3   Stay straight/left at the intersection with the Metolius–Windigo Trail, which takes off to the right.

14.4   At the intersection with Found Lake Trail, stay right.

14.9   You'll T into the Charlton Lake Trail/Metolius–Windigo Trail here. Turn left to go to Charlton Lake.

16.2   Start riding alongside Charlton Lake, which will be to your right.

16.8   Check out the nice swimming spot at Charlton Lake. From here, take the trail that goes to Waldo Lake. You will cross the PCT soon, but continue toward Waldo Lake.

17.0   Cross graveled Charlton Lake Rd.
17.2   Cross FR 5897.
18.1   Cross FR 5898.
18.4   Turn right on the Waldo Lake Trail, heading north.
19.0   Return to North Waldo Campground and day-use area for the end of
the ride.

OPTIONS

This ride can be done in either direction. Also, if you are looking for a very
long ride, tag on the Lemish and Charlton lakes loop (see Route 24), the
Waldo Lake loop (see Route 23), or both. Plan for a very long day in the saddle
if that is what you choose.

27 MAIDEN PEAK

OUT-AND-BACK

Trail Type: 100% singletrack
Distance: 12.2 miles
Elevation Gain/Loss: 3170/3170 feet
High Point: 7801 feet
Ride Time: 3–4 hours
Technical Difficulty: Advanced
Fitness Intensity: Very strenuous

Season: July–October
Map: Adventure Maps, Oakridge,
Oregon Trail Map
GPS: 43.6257° N, -122.0464° W
Land Managers: Willamette National
Forest; Deschutes National Forest

OVERVIEW

This out-and-back, at just over 12 miles total, is one heck of a steep ride.
You'll spend the majority of your time climbing before bombing down to the
bottom again. The downhill is an absolute scream, though, with much of it
on smooth, fall-line trail. It's also a wonderful ride for getting sublime views
of Waldo Lake, Odell Lake, Diamond Peak, and additional volcanic peaks in
the distance.

The ride follows the Maiden Peak Trail the whole way and climbs con-
sistently and very steeply at times. The trail surface usually has enough traction for about three-quarters of the ride before giving way to looser, steeper

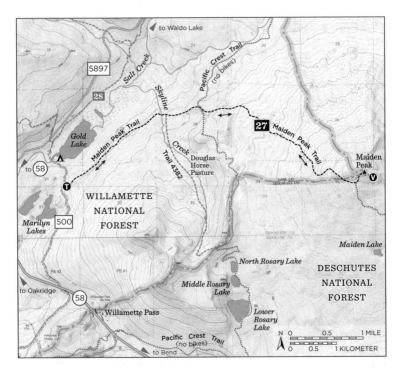

terrain: most people walk their bikes to the summit. Like so many other peaks in the area, the summit is loose red cinders, the signature of ancient Cascade volcanoes.

GETTING THERE

From Bend, take US Highway 97 South until you reach the Crescent Cutoff Road (County Road 61) in the town of Crescent (there is a Shell gas station on the corner). Turn right here. In another 24 miles, turn right onto Oregon Route 58. About a half mile past the Willamette Pass ski area, turn right on unpaved Forest Road 500 (Gold Lake Road). Follow this road 1.6 miles until you reach the Maiden Peak trailhead on your right.

MILEAGE LOG

0.0 From the Maiden Peak trailhead, get on the Maiden Peak Trail. You'll start climbing right away, but the first 2 miles aren't quite as steep as the rest, so relish the relatively relaxed grade for a little while.

2.0 Trail 4382 takes off to the right, heading to Douglas Horse Pasture. Stay straight on the Maiden Peak Trail.

3.5 The Pacific Crest Trail (PCT), which is closed to bikes, crosses here. Stay straight.

5.9 This hiker-only trail to the right drops to Maiden Lake; you are almost to the top of Maiden Peak.

6.1 At the top of Maiden Peak, enjoy the views, then descend back the way you came when you are ready.

8.7 Cross the PCT, and stay on Maiden Peak Trail.

10.2 Stay straight at the intersection with Trail 4382.

12.2 Return to the trailhead where you parked your car.

Descending off the top of Maiden Peak (Photo: Melanie Fisher)

28 MOUNT RAY AND FUJI MOUNTAIN

LOOP

Trail Type: 100% singletrack

Distance: 14.3 miles

Elevation Gain/Loss: 2270/2270 feet

High Point: 6590 feet

Ride Time: 3–4 hours

Technical Difficulty: Advanced

Fitness Intensity: Strenuous

Season: July–October

Map: Adventure Maps, Oakridge, Oregon Trail Map

GPS: 43.6297° N, -122.0485° W

Land Manager: Willamette National Forest

OVERVIEW

The Mount Ray to Fuji Mountain loop is another great ride to add on to a weekend of riding in the Waldo Lake region. You won't see many people out here, as it's tough and steep and a little off the radar. Although it can be ridden when the snow is clear, I recommend doing this in late August, or even later, when you're less likely to encounter swarms of mosquitoes. This ride has a little of everything including big trees, creeks, lakes, meadows, and a western Cascades peak.

You'll start at Gold Lake, another lovely swimming hole surrounded by tall fir and hemlock trees. The first part of the route follows the Gold Lake Trail to the north, paralleling paved Forest Road 5897, so you have the option of riding on pavement instead, if you wish. You'll then take the trail up the steep Ray Creek drainage, paralleling the Waldo Lake Wilderness, into the high country. You don't actually get too close to Mount Ray, but you do have the option (described below) to make the 1.6-mile climb up Fuji Mountain.

GETTING THERE

From Bend, take US Highway 97 South until you reach the Crescent Cutoff Road (County Road 61) in the town of Crescent (there is a Shell gas station on the corner). Turn right here. In another 24 miles, turn right onto Oregon Route 58. About a half mile past the Willamette Pass ski area, turn right on unpaved Forest Road 500 (Gold Lake Road). Follow this road 2 miles until

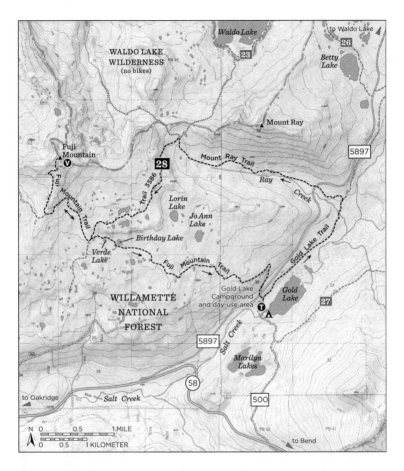

you reach the Gold Lake Campground and day-use area. Park here for the start of the ride.

MILEAGE LOG

0.0 From Gold Lake Campground and day-use area, head north on the Gold Lake Trail. *Option: This trail parallels paved FR 5897 if you want to take that instead.*

Look for the US Geological Survey marker on Fuji Mountain. (Photo: Charlie Biggs)

2.0 Turn left on the Mount Ray Trail.

2.5 Cross FR 5897. Continue on the trail, climbing up the Ray Creek drainage. It's a steep one, so get comfortable and settle in!

4.9 At the four-way intersection, turn left onto Trail 3586. Straight and right both lead into the Waldo Lake Wilderness, which is closed to bikes.

7.3 After riding through varied terrain with some little lakes along the way, you'll reach the intersection for Fuji Mountain. Turn right here to climb up to Fuji. *Option: If you don't want to make the steep climb to Fuji, turn left on the Fuji Mountain Trail to return to Gold Lake.*

8.3 Watch for this tricky intersection and be sure to stay to the right to continue up to Fuji Mountain. Left will lead you onto a dirt road and strand you off-route.

8.9 After some super steep switchbacks, you'll reach the summit of Fuji Mountain. Turn around when you've had enough of the killer views.

9.5 Turn left at this intersection to descend the Fuji Mountain Trail.

10.5 At this four-way intersection, stay straight on the Fuji Mountain Trail. Just past the intersection will be Verde Lake and Birthday Lake. From here, it's almost all downhill back to the trailhead. It's a fun one.

14.2 Cross paved FR 5897.

14.3 Return to Gold Lake Campground and day-use area.

OPTIONS

You can connect this ride with the Waldo Lake Trail (see Route 23) for an epic summertime ride. Do this by riding either paved FR 5897 or the Gold Lake Trail (it runs parallel to FR 5897, on the east side of the road) north toward the Betty Lake Trail.

EAST AND SOUTH OF BEND

Oregon's high desert is the geographic area extending from Bend to the south and the east—all the way to the borders of California, Nevada, and Idaho. The Horse Ridge, Horse Butte, and Swamp Wells rides (Routes 29–31) are representative of the classic high-desert geology, with trails that travel through wide-open sage punctuated by distinct lava rock formations. The Newberry Caldera ride (Route 34), Deschutes River Trail (Route 32), and Black Rock Trail (Route 33), all farther to the south, expose you even more intimately to the volcanic landscape, with views of massive lava flows originating from the Newberry Volcano.

The eastern trails, specifically those in the Horse Ridge and Horse Butte areas, can be good options for winter riding if there is no, or very little, snow on the ground. Just watch for the freeze-thaw cycle. Riding during these messy and muddy conditions causes lasting damage to the trails.

These rides wind through open cattle range, so be sure to leave any cattle gates as you find them. If they are closed, close them again behind you. If you find them open, keep them open.

Opposite: *Follow the ribbon of dirt at the Horse Butte trails.*

29 HORSE RIDGE

LOOP

Trail Type: 75% singletrack, 20% pavement, 5% dirt road
Distance: 12.0 miles
Elevation Gain/Loss: 1450/1450 feet
High Point: 4887 feet
Ride Time: 2–3 hours
Technical Difficulty: Advanced
Fitness Intensity: Moderate

Season: Year-round, best in winter and spring
Map: Adventure Maps, Bend, Oregon Trail Map
GPS: 43.9460° N, -121.0435° W
Land Manager: Bureau of Land Management, Prineville District

OVERVIEW

Most of the winter and early spring mountain biking in Bend is mild, with smooth, buffed-out trails. Horse Ridge is the exception to that. It is rocky and rough in places, and has significant elevation gain. As an early season ride, the steep grade is a bit of a wake-up call! It's also a gorgeous ride through old junipers mixed with sage and native grasses, with huge views.

Horse Ridge was not necessarily intended to be a mountain biking area historically; but when a group of riders and trail builders started scratching in some trails, it quickly became popular as a winter/spring trail network. On a sunny day in February, when the trails are free of snow, you might see a lot of cars in the parking lot. Locals are itching to take a break from skiing and get on their bikes to pedal.

Climbing up a switchback on Horse Ridge
(Photo: Heidi Faller)

The BLM is working directly with the Central Oregon Trail Alliance (COTA) and other trail users to officially designate these trails; but be aware that there may be changes and reroutes in the future. You'll notice that you will climb over at least two barbed wire fences. These fences mark the boundaries of the Horse Ridge Research Natural Area, 600 acres designated in 1967 as a research and study plot for western juniper and big sagebrush plant communities. There is a slight chance that some of the trails may be closed or rerouted, but the BLM reassures us that mountain bikers will still be able to access great new trails in the vicinity.

Pay close attention to tread conditions, especially in the winter. Due to its elevation, this area can hold snow for a long while, and it is also susceptible to the mucky freeze-thaw cycle. If you aren't sure about trail conditions, ask at a local bike shop.

GETTING THERE

From the intersection of NE 3rd Street and NE Greenwood Avenue in Bend, take Greenwood Avenue east to where it turns into US Highway 20. Continue on US 20 for 16.8 miles until you reach Horse Ridge Frontage Road (Old Highway 20) just before the top of the big hill. Take a sharp right on this paved road and drive for 0.7 mile until you see a gravel parking lot and trailhead on your left. Park here.

MILEAGE LOG

0.0 From the gravel parking lot and trailhead, go through the gate and take the trail to your immediate left. Stay on this trail to parallel the Horse Ridge Frontage Rd., then the highway, both to your left. This section is rolly, but mostly uphill.

1.9 At the top of the hill, stay straight on the trail to continue alongside the road. *Option: The trail to your right is Parkway, and if you want to climb up it, go for it. It is a shorter ride, but a harder climb up the technical singletrack.*

2.0 When you reach the old highway, continue on it (straight). This is Old Hwy. 20, which is paved, but rough in places. It is mostly uphill, with some rollers.

4.4 At the top of this hill, look for a trail on your right. Take this trail, called Has No Horse, up toward the top of Horse Ridge. Expect a few rocks, but much of the way is smooth.

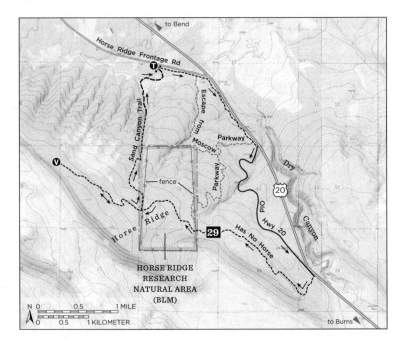

6.6 Climb over the barbed wire fence. Immediately to your right, Parkway Trail heads down. To the left/straight, Has No Horse continues along the ridge. *Option: For a shorter ride, take Parkway back down to your car. It's a great trail with a lot of challenging rock gardens.*

7.6 Carry your bike over the second fence crossing. Immediately past the fence, Sand Canyon Trail heads downhill to the right. *Option: At this point, you can descend Sand Canyon back to your car.* To continue along the ridge (recommended), stay straight. The ridge gradually climbs with easy to moderate rock gardens along the way.

9.0 You've reached the end of the trail and the high point on Horse Ridge. Enjoy the big-sky views from here! When you are ready, turn around and head back on the trail that you were on.

10.4 At the intersection with Sand Canyon Trail, turn left to ride down Sand Canyon.

11.2 The trail emerges from the canyon and turns into a dirt road. Follow this all the way back to the parking area.

12.0 Return to your car.

OPTIONS

I've suggested this route that includes the paved road to give you the longest option for a loop ride. But you can ride these trails any way you like, including riding up and down Parkway or Escape from Moscow. I don't recommend riding up Sand Canyon. It's steep, and the risk of (literally) running into downhill riders is high during peak riding season.

30 HORSE BUTTE

LOOP

Trail Type: 80% singletrack, 20% dirt road

Distance: 12.8 miles

Elevation Gain/Loss: 760/760 feet

High Point: 4412 feet

Ride Time: 1–2 hours

Technical Difficulty: Intermediate

Fitness Intensity: Moderate

Season: Year-round, depending on the winter

Map: Adventure Maps, Bend, Oregon Trail Map

GPS: 43.9743° N, -121.2297° W

Land Manager: Deschutes National Forest

OVERVIEW

The Horse Butte area is a fantastic winter and early spring riding area if there is no snow on the ground. These trails are fast and fun, with wide-open, 360-degree views of the high desert and the Cascades. The area was the site of a large forest fire, the Skeleton Fire, in 1996, so there aren't many live large trees, and it can be quite windy. It's also a popular running and dog walking area—and you'll encounter the occasional horseback rider—so share the trails; a little friendliness goes a long way. There are some cool lava caves out here, but unfortunately most of them are closed off due to vandalism issues. If you want to visit the caves, check with the Deschutes National Forest first.

During the winter and spring months, this area can be very muddy thanks to freeze-thaw cycles. Please stay off the trails when they are wet because tire tracks in mud eventually lead to ruts; a way to do this is to ride very early in the morning when the ground is still frozen (making this trail extra fast!).

This loop is fun in either direction, but I've written it up here in counterclockwise fashion. To add a few more miles, I've included a section of gravel road; for a little bit shorter loop, you can stay on singletrack the whole time.

GETTING THERE

From the intersection of NE 3rd Street and NE Greenwood Avenue in Bend, take Greenwood Avenue (which turns into US Highway 20) east 2 miles to

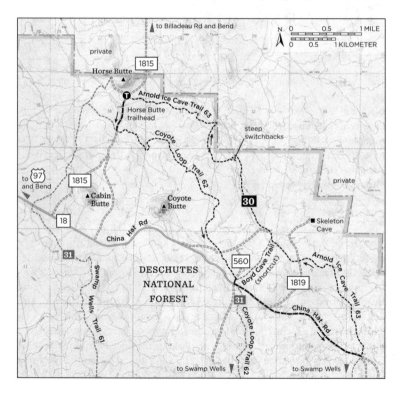

A blue-sky day in the high desert on the Horse Butte loop

SE 27th Street. Turn right onto SE 27th Street and drive 3.2 miles to turn left onto Rickard Road. In another 1.8 miles, turn right onto Billadeau Road, heading south until it turns into Forest Road 1815. Continue to the parking area on the right, just past the red cinder Horse Butte.

MILEAGE LOG

0.0   Start at the Horse Butte trailhead. Turn right onto dirt FR 1815 and ride south for 0.5 mile.

0.5   Turn left onto Coyote Loop Trail 62.

4.1   Turn right on red cinder FR 560. This is a quick jog to China Hat Rd. *Option: If you cross the road onto the Boyd Cave Trail, you can do a shorter loop.*

4.2   Turn left onto China Hat Rd. This is a busy dirt road, so be careful and watch for cars.

6.4   Turn left onto Arnold Ice Cave Trail 63. *Option: If you were to turn right on this trail, you would head toward Swamp Wells (see Route 31).*

8.9   Stay right on Arnold Ice Cave Trail. The trail to the left is the shortcut mentioned in mile 4.1. From here, you'll ride close to private property in the Sundance neighborhood. These trails are loved by the neighbors, so keep an eye out for runners and walkers.

10.2 Watch for a loose and rocky set of switchbacks here.

12.8 Return to the Horse Butte trailhead.

31   SWAMP WELLS

LOOP

Trail Type: 100% singletrack
Distance: 26 miles
Elevation Gain/Loss: 2050/2050 feet
High Point: 5507 feet
Ride Time: 3–4 hours
Technical Difficulty: Intermediate
Fitness Intensity: Strenuous

Season: April–October
Map: Adventure Maps, Bend, Oregon Trail Map
GPS: 43.9743° N, -121.2297° W
Land Manager: Deschutes National Forest

OVERVIEW

This ride combines part of the Horse Butte ride (see Route 30) with the section of Swamp Wells Trail that climbs up the north side of the gently sloping Newberry Volcano. Routefinding can be challenging, so take your time to get your bearings at intersections, which are mostly unmarked. Much of the ride goes through classic pine tree forest, which shields the views; but there are some excellent views from the section that traverses Kelsey Butte. From there you can see Mount Bachelor, Broken Top, and South, Middle, and North Sister, as well as Mount Jefferson and, on a

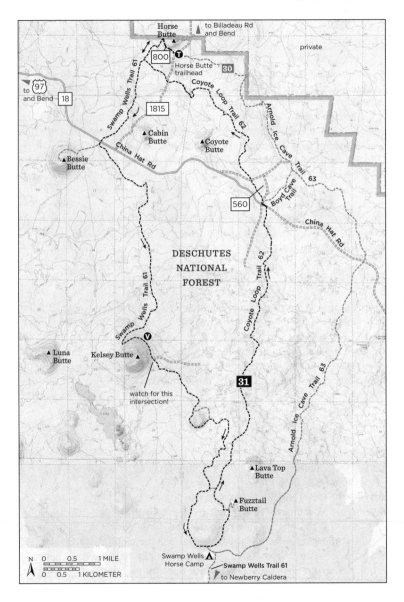

Horse Butte

to Billadeau Rd and Bend

private

800 **T**

Swamp Wells Trail 61

Horse Butte trailhead

30

97 to and Bend **18**

Coyote Loop Trail 62

1815

▲ Cabin Butte

▲ Coyote Butte

Arnold Ice Cave Trail 63

China Hat Rd

▲ Bessie Butte

560

Boyd Cave Trail

China Hat Rd

DESCHUTES NATIONAL FOREST

Coyote Loop Trail 62

Swamp Wells Trail 61

V

▲ Luna Butte

Kelsey Butte ▲

31

watch for this intersection!

Arnold Ice Cave Trail 63

▲ Lava Top Butte

▲ Fuzztail Butte

N

0   0.5   1 MILE

0   0.5   1 KILOMETER

Swamp Wells Horse Camp ▲

Swamp Wells Trail 61
to Newberry Caldera

super clear day, Mount Hood. You can also spot Smith Rock and Lookout Mountain in the Ochocos.

There are actually three trails to choose from, and they can be ridden either up or down. I recommend taking the Swamp Wells Trail up and the Coyote Loop Trail down. The third option is the Arnold Ice Cave Trail, which is farthest to the east.

The trick to hitting this ride at the right time is to get on it right after it is cleared of snow and downed trees but before the equestrians start using it. It can get loose, dusty, and bumpy from horse hooves. Late April or early May is usually good, or very late in fall if we've had significant rain to give the tread some tackiness and keep the dust down. The campground at Swamp Wells is largely a horse camp, so you may see a few horseback riders.

To get a full-on, epic ride on these trails, ride the Newberry Caldera loop (see Route 34), then instead of completing the last few miles, turn onto the Swamp Wells Trail and descend to Horse Butte. You'll need to arrange a shuttle for that, but it's a solid ride.

GETTING THERE

From the intersection of NE 3rd Street and NE Greenwood Avenue in Bend, take Greenwood Avenue (which turns into US Highway 20) east 2 miles to SE 27th Street. Turn right onto SE 27th Street and drive 3.2 miles to turn left onto Rickard Road. In another 1.8 miles, turn right onto Billadeau Road, heading south until it turns into Forest Road 1815. Continue to the parking area on the right, just past the red cinder Horse Butte.

MILEAGE LOG

0.0   From the Horse Butte trailhead, take dirt FR 800 west toward Swamp Wells Trail 61.

0.3   Turn left onto Swamp Wells Trail.

0.8   At the intersection with Coyote Loop Trail 62, stay straight and continue on Swamp Wells Trail.

2.6   Cross China Hat Rd. and stay on Swamp Wells Trail.

6.9   The trail will get steeper as you start to climb up Kelsey Butte. Once the trail flattens out and traverses the north side of the butte, check out the lovely views of the Cascades and the high desert.

8.3   Pay attention here! As you wrap around Kelsey Butte, the trail turns into an old dirt road. Look to your right for a singletrack heading up.

Mount Bachelor and the Three Sisters provide the backdrop to the Kelsey Butte section of the Swamp Wells ride.

Routefinding is tricky because you are likely to bomb right down the road. Instead, take the trail to the right.

9.7 The trail splits here, but it comes together after wrapping around either side of a little butte. The trail to the left is super rocky and challenging. The trail to the right is not rocky, but is narrowed by manzanita bushes.

12.3 At this intersection, stay straight toward Swamp Wells.

13.8 You are now just north of Swamp Wells Horse Camp. Continue around another butte on what is now the Coyote Loop Trail.

14.6 At the intersection for Fuzztail Butte, stay left on Coyote Loop Trail. From here, you'll descend for most of the second half of the ride.

15.3 Stay right at this intersection and continue on Coyote Loop Trail. After this, you'll cross a few dirt roads, but you'll stay on this trail. Watch for horses along this section.

21.2 When you reach China Hat Rd., turn left, then take a quick right onto FR 560 to get on the trail again. The Boyd Cave Trail will veer to the right, but stay left on the Coyote Loop Trail.

24.8 Cross dirt FR 1815.

25.2 Turn right on Swamp Wells Trail.

25.7 Turn right on graveled FR 800.

26.0 Return to where you parked your car at the Horse Butte trailhead.

32 DESCHUTES RIVER TRAIL

OUT-AND-BACK

Trail Type: 95% singletrack, 5% dirt road
Distance: 23 miles
Elevation Gain/Loss: 1080/1080 feet
High Point: 4205 feet
Ride Time: 1–4 hours
Technical Difficulty: Intermediate
Fitness Intensity: Easy–strenuous

Season: April–November
Map: Adventure Maps, Bend, Oregon Trail Map
GPS: 43.9972° N, -121.385° W
Land Manager: Deschutes National Forest
Permit: NW Forest Pass (annual or day pass), May 1–September 30

OVERVIEW

Originating at the high lakes and running to the Columbia River, the Deschutes River is the main waterway in central Oregon. The Deschutes River Trail is a lovely ride that stays close to the river the whole way. It is a very loved trail by hikers, trail runners, mountain bikers, and casual walkers and is the go-to place for the Bend and Sunriver tourist crowd, so it can get crowded. That said, I make a point of getting on the river trail every fall when I know the colors will be good. There are some nice aspen stands and verges of dogwood and other local shrubbery that make for a pretty fall ride.

The Deschutes River Trail runs from the Meadow picnic area all the

The Deschutes River Trail is a cruiser out-and-back ride. (Photo: Chris Kratsch)

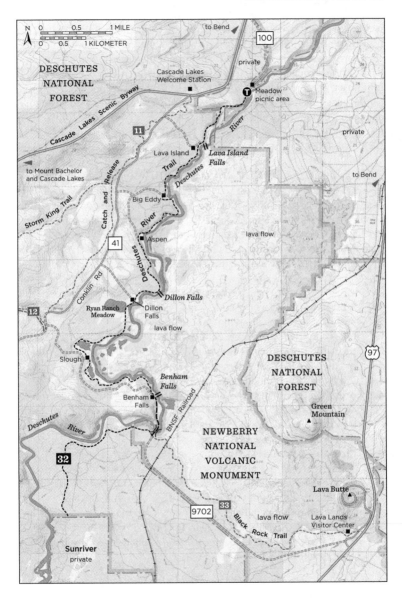

way south to Sunriver, with three significant cascading waterfalls along the way. In total, the trail is 11.5 miles one way, but you can go as far as you wish, then turn around whenever you like. At all of the day-use areas, you might have to ride through gravel parking areas to find the trail on the other side. It is quite easy to find the trail, so just take a careful look around.

Because this trail is an out-and-back, I've noted it as easy to strenuous, depending on how far you want to ride.

GETTING THERE

From the intersection of NE 3rd Street and NE Greenwood Avenue in Bend, take Greenwood Avenue west. In 1.5 miles, at the roundabout, turn left to head south on NW 14th Street, which eventually turns into Cascade Lakes Scenic Byway. Continue on Cascade Lakes Scenic Byway and in 5.1 miles, just before Widgi Golf Course, turn left onto dirt Forest Road 100. Follow this road for 1.3 miles to its end at the Meadow picnic area. Between May 1 and September 30, this trailhead requires a Northwest Forest Pass.

MILEAGE LOG

0.0 Start at the Meadow picnic area, and get on the Deschutes River Trail at the far end of the parking area.

1.4 Cross the Lava Island Falls day-use area.

2.7 Cross the Big Eddy day-use area. This is a popular river rafting section of the Deschutes, so you might see some rafts floating downstream.

3.4 Cross the Aspen day-use area.

4.8 Cross the Dillon Falls day-use area, with nice views of the river from a high plateau. Right after Dillon Falls, you will ride through Ryan Ranch Meadow, a pretty meadow with Mount Bachelor peeking out through the surrounding treetops.

6.6 Cross the Slough day-use area.

8.0 You are now at the uppermost and most popular waterfall, Benham Falls, where you will likely encounter a fair number of tourists. From here, the trail turns into a dirt road until you cross the river.

8.7 At the top of Benham Falls, cross the river on the wooden bridge and continue on the Deschutes River Trail. *Option: The Black Rock Trail starts here, to the left. To add 8.2 miles, follow it to Lava Butte and back (see Route 33).*

11.5 You've reached the northern border of Sunriver, a popular tourist and resort community. This is the end of the Deschutes River Trail. Turn around and follow the river all the way back.

14.3 Cross the river.

15.0 You are back at Benham Falls, so watch for hikers. Retrace your single-track route, crossing through the several day-use areas along the way.

23.0 Return back to your car at Meadow picnic area.

33 BLACK ROCK TRAIL

OUT-AND-BACK

Trail Type: 100% singletrack
Distance: 8.2 miles
Elevation Gain/Loss: 500/500 feet
High Point: 4501 feet
Ride Time: 1–2 hours

Technical Difficulty: Beginner
Fitness Intensity: Easy
Season: May–October
Map: Adventure Maps, Bend, Oregon Trail Map

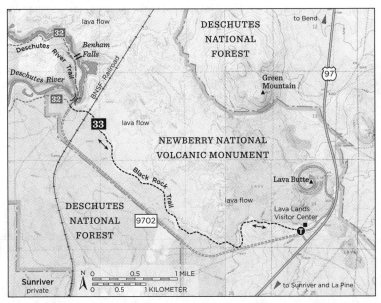

GPS: 43.9095° N, -121.3597° W
Land Manager: Newberry National Volcanic Monument, Deschutes National Forest

Permit: NW Forest Pass (annual or day pass) or Newberry National Volcanic Monument Pass, May 1– September 30

OVERVIEW

The Black Rock Trail connects Lava Butte to the Deschutes River and runs right alongside the Lava Butte lava flow, seven square miles of lava that flowed from the base of Lava Butte over 7000 years ago. The trail is mellow, with very few technical features, and is a nice ride for a beginner rider or a family with kids. It is 4.1 miles from Lava Butte to the Deschutes River just above Benham Falls. This can be combined with a jaunt on the Deschutes River Trail (see Route 32), either up- or downriver, if you are looking for more.

I also recommend checking out the Lava Lands Visitor Center with its cool displays and trails that wind through the lava. I worked here in the late 1990s, and the interpretive displays and programs have improved so much over the last twenty years. You'll be amazed at the geologic wonderland that is central Oregon!

Bikepacking on the Black Rock Trail

GETTING THERE

From Bend, drive south on US Highway 97 for about 11 miles, until you reach Lava Butte. You can't miss this red cinder hill just to the right of the highway. Turn right into the Lava Lands Visitor Center and park here.

MILEAGE LOG

0.0   Starting at the Lava Lands Visitor Center, get on the Black Rock Trail.

3.9   Cross the railroad tracks.

4.1   Cross FR 9702. You're at the Deschutes River. Turn around here to retrace your ride. *Option: To get more miles in, you can choose to ride upriver toward Sunriver or downriver toward Bend along the Deschutes River Trail (see Route 32).*

4.3   Recross the railroad tracks.

8.2   Return to the Lava Lands Visitor Center.

34 NEWBERRY CALDERA

LOOP

Trail Type: 80% singletrack, 20% dirt road
Distance: 22.6 miles
Elevation Gain/Loss: 3380/ 3380 feet
High Point: 7963 feet
Ride Time: 3–5 hours
Technical Difficulty: Advanced
Fitness Intensity: Very strenuous
Season: July–October

Map: Adventure Maps, Bend, Oregon Trail Map
GPS: 43.7122° N, -121.2759° W
Land Manager: Newberry National Volcanic Monument, Deschutes National Forest
Permit: NW Forest Pass (annual or day pass) or Newberry National Volcanic Monument Pass, May 1–September 30

OVERVIEW

How many times have you ridden around an ancient volcano caldera dotted with two of the bluest of lakes? The Newberry Caldera loop gives you the opportunity to do a tough ride through some spectacular geology around Paulina and East lakes. This is a remote, high-elevation ride with virtually

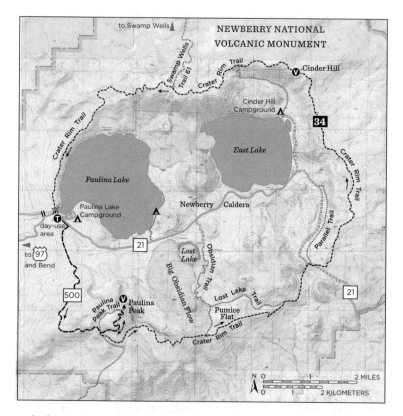

no bailout points, so it is only for strong, experienced mountain bikers. The route includes a steep gravel road climb and loose, steep downhill sections. This is also a multiuse trail; please watch for and be respectful of hikers and equestrians, especially on the north and west sides of the lakes. Be sure to check on snowpack and blowdown conditions before you go.

GETTING THERE

From Bend, drive south on US Highway 97 for 23 miles. Turn left onto paved Forest Road 21 and follow this 12.5 miles to Newberry National Volcanic Monument and Paulina Lake. You'll pass a guard station on your way into

Overlooking the massive Big Obsidian Flow and East Lake at Newberry Caldera
(Photo: Derek Faller)

the monument where you can buy a day pass, which you must have to ride in the monument. Park at the day-use area next to Paulina Lake Campground. There is a kiosk here where you can purchase a day pass if the guard station is closed.

MILEAGE LOG

0.0 From the day-use area at Paulina Lake, turn back left onto paved FR 21 upon leaving the parking lot.

0.2 Turn right onto FR 500, the steep gravel road that goes to Paulina Peak. This climb starts steep and sustains, so settle in. Watch out for car traffic, as this is a popular day trip to Paulina Peak.

3.4 Keep an eye out for the trail to your right that drops down off the road. You'll be coming back here after you climb up to the Paulina Peak overlook. *Option: If you want to skip the overlook (I don't recommend it, you'll miss a gorgeous view), this is your starting point on the trail.*

4.4 The overlook at Paulina Peak has an awesome view of the lakes and the massive Big Obsidian Flow. From here, turn around and ride back down the road 1 mile to the trail.

5.4 The trail, Crater Rim Trail, is hard to see when you are descending the road, so go slow and watch carefully for it! After turning left onto the trail, the first part is steep and technical with loose rocks and tight switchbacks.

5.5 At the intersection with Paulina Peak Trail, stay left on Crater Rim Trail.

8.0 The hiker-only trail down to the Big Obsidian Flow takes off to the left. Stay straight on Crater Rim Trail.

9.0 You'll drop down a very loose, pumice-laden downhill, with some big water bars. It's pretty fun if you can keep from sliding out.

9.8 At the intersection with the hiker-only Lost Lake Trail, stay right on Crater Rim Trail.

10.9 Cross dirt FR 21. This is the only real bailout point on the ride, and it is still a long way back to the car on this road. Stay on Crater Rim Trail. From here, the trail gets wide and rolly, with a lot of ups and downs.

14.5 After a steep uphill, you'll come to red Cinder Hill with spectacular views of the lakes. Take a break and fuel up, because there is more climbing ahead.

16.5 At the intersection with the hiker-only trail down to Cinder Hill Campground and East Lake, stay straight on Crater Rim Trail.

18.2 At the junction with Swamp Wells Trail 61, stay straight on Crater Rim Trail. *Epic option: This is an epic ride-to-town option for another day. Swamp Wells Trail connects to the Coyote Loop Trail, which eventually connects to the southeast edge of Bend. Do not do this unless you are well prepared for a very long day, and you have arranged a shuttle.*

18.6 You're done climbing! The trail descends very steeply with very large water bars, roots and rocks, and some loose switchbacks. Be careful! Also keep an eye out for equestrians and hikers, as this is a popular section of trail for all users.

21.0 The downhill mellows out a bit as you continue to parallel the west shore of Paulina Lake.

22.6 Cross the bridge and ride back to your car, parked at the day-use area at Paulina Lake Campground.

CROOK COUNTY AND OCHOCO MOUNTAINS

If you are looking to visit the next up-and-coming mountain bike mecca, Crook County should be on your list. The little community of Prineville has worked very hard to revitalize old trails and develop new mountain-bike-specific trails in the area. Prineville is about an hour's drive from Bend, so it makes for a reasonable day trip or a great weekend getaway. One of the newest mountain biking zones in central Oregon is right in town: although tiny, as just under 3 miles, the Lower 66 trail network (Route 35) is a great stop for a quick spin.

The Central Oregon Trail Alliance (COTA) also completed a bike park in Prineville in summer 2016, adding another option for biking in the area. Learn more about the bike park at the COTA Crook County Chapter webpage: www.cotamtb.com/chapters/crook-county.

The Ochoco Mountains just east of Prineville are actually part of the Blue Mountains, which are some of the oldest mountains in the Northwest. The trails in the Ochoco Mountains are multiuse, but have become more popular with mountain bikers over the years. Expect to see horseback riders and a number of all-terrain vehicles and motorcycles on the dirt roads. Round and Lookout mountains are just gorgeous in the early summer when the native grasses are green and the wildflowers start blooming. You also get fabulous views of central Oregon in its entirety. Watch for summer thunderstorms, however, as these mountains are very exposed to any weather that comes along.

Opposite: *A rider makes her way across Lookout Mountain in the Ochocos.* (Photo: Tim Kaiser)

Ochoco Brewing Company is the local pub and grub favorite, serving microbrews and burgers made with local eastern Oregon beef. Good Bike Co. is a wonderful little bike shop that serves the community and always has up-to-date information on trail conditions. Good Bike Co. also has local beer on tap, so belly up to the bar for a post-ride drink!

35 LOWER 66

NETWORK

Trail Type: 100% singletrack
Distance: Up to 2.5 miles
Elevation Gain/Loss: 350/350 feet
High Point: 3068 feet
Ride Time: 30 minutes–1 hour
Technical Difficulty: Intermediate
Fitness Intensity: Easy

Season: Almost year-round
Map: Online at www.cotamtb.com /2014/lower-66-project-2
GPS: 44.2966° N, -120.8668° W
Land Manager: Oregon Parks and Recreation Department

One of the fun skill-building features at Lower 66 (Photo: Travis Holman)

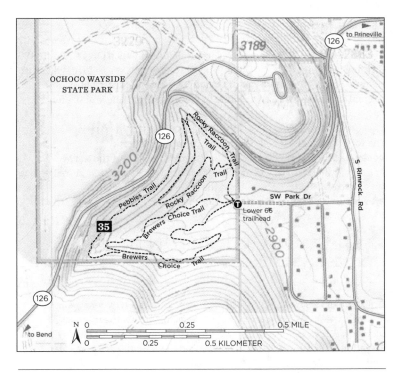

OVERVIEW

Yes, at under 3 miles, the Lower 66 trails may seem like a strange addition to this guidebook. However, this area is a significant milestone for mountain biking in Prineville. Unlike Bend, Prineville has not historically been a mountain biking mecca, and the community desperately needed access to a trail network that was easy to get to from town. The Crook County Chapter of COTA, working diligently with the Oregon Parks and Recreation Department and the Prineville community, developed this small patch of singletrack that is now very well loved by locals. There are more trails in store for this area, so be sure to check back.

These short loops can be ridden in either direction or lapped to get more mileage. There are some surprisingly narrow, technical sections that provide opportunities for a good challenge.

GETTING THERE

From Bend, take US Highway 97 North to Redmond, then Oregon Route 126 East toward Prineville. In 17.6 miles, just before you get to Prineville, turn right at South Rimrock Road. In another 0.3 mile, turn right at SW Park Drive. Take SW Park Drive 0.3 mile to the end and park here at the fence.

MILEAGE LOG

The following trails are all part of the Lower 66 network:

Rocky Raccoon Trail: 1.0 mile; the northernmost loop of the network.

Pebbles Trail: 0.5 mile; the narrowest, most technical section of trail, taking you to the highest elevation in the network.

Brewers Choice Trail: 1.0 mile; the southernmost loop.

36 LOOKOUT MOUNTAIN

LOOP

Trail Type: 55% singletrack, 45% pavement, 5% dirt road

Distance: 18.5 miles

Elevation Gain/Loss: 3470/3470 feet

High Point: 6918 feet

Ride Time: 3–5 hours

Technical Difficulty: Advanced–expert

Fitness Intensity: Very strenuous

Season: July–October

Map: Adventure Maps, Sisters & Redmond High Desert Trail Map

GPS: 44.3962° N, -120.4258° W

Land Manager: Ochoco National Forest

OVERVIEW

Lookout Mountain is the highest point in the Ochoco Mountains and it always delivers excitement. Years ago, this was a popular area for sheepherders, which also meant sheepdogs who occasionally liked to chase bikes. I haven't seen any sheep out here in recent years, but I've seen a black bear and elk and have encountered the sudden summer thunderstorm, making it an adventurous outing each time.

Don't be turned away by the paved road climb on this ride. It is an okay road ride, with sparse traffic, and serves as a good warm-up for what's to come. Once you get on the trail, you continue to climb up to the wide plateau

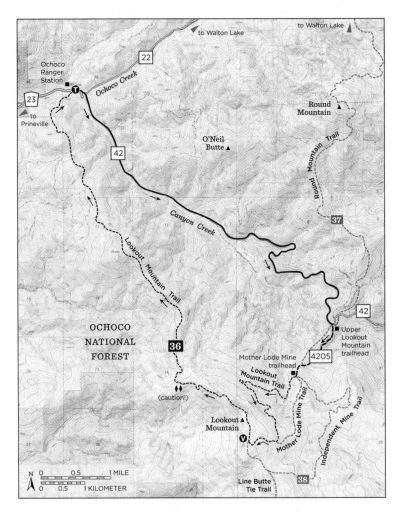

of Lookout Mountain. It is a spectacular view from here, and if you hit it right in the summer, you'll find plenty of wildflowers. The descent off the top of Lookout Mountain is one of the gnarliest downhills around. (This is why I've noted the technical difficulty as advanced to expert.) The top couple of miles

Lookout Mountain has superb wildflowers if you catch it at the right time.
(Photo: Cog Wild)

are very rocky, very tight, and very steep, with some expert-only switchbacks. The last 6 miles are pure downhill bliss, interspersed with three fairly short climbs. You'll be feeling them when you get there.

GETTING THERE

From the intersection of US Highway 26 (NE 3rd Street) and Main Street in downtown Prineville, take US 26 East. In 16 miles, stay right on Ochoco Creek Road (County Road 23). In another 5 miles, stay right again on Ochoco Ranger Road (CR 23). In 3.2 miles, turn left into the Ochoco Ranger Station and rental cabins. Park here. Across the road you will see the Lookout Mountain Trail, which you will be coming down at the end of the ride.

MILEAGE LOG

0.0 Start at the Ochoco Ranger Station and cabins. Take Ochoco Ranger Rd. (CR 23) east.

0.1 Turn right onto paved FR 42. Climb up this paved road for about 7 miles.

7.3 Turn right onto dirt FR 4205 at the Upper Lookout Mountain trailhead. Continue climbing. There is a trail to the right of the road, but it is very steep. I recommend riding the road.

8.3 At the Mother Lode Mine trailhead, three trails take off. I recommend you take the Lookout Mountain Trail, which is to the right. The Independent Mine Trail, the trail farthest left, is a mile longer but also a good option. The trail in the middle, the Mother Lode Mine Trail, is incredibly steep.

10.5 Here, the Lookout Mountain Trail and the Mother Lode Mine Trail converge. Continue on Lookout Mountain Trail.

11.1 You're at the top of Lookout Mountain, an open plateau. Enjoy the views, then continue north on the Lookout Mountain Trail across the big plateau. Once you start descending, you'll get into the hard stuff— extremely steep, rocky switchbacks. Most riders walk their bikes at some point.

12.5 You're through the hard stuff, and now the trail continues to roll downhill with some brief climbing interludes. Watch for equestrians.

18.5 Return to your car at the Ochoco Ranger Station.

37 ROUND AND LOOKOUT MOUNTAINS EPIC

LOOP

Trail Type: 70% singletrack, 25% pavement, 5% dirt road
Distance: 28.7 miles
Elevation Gain/Loss: 5470/5470 feet
High Point: 6918 feet
Ride Time: 4–6 hours
Technical Difficulty: Advanced–expert

Fitness Intensity: Very strenuous
Season: July–October
Map: Adventure Maps, Sisters & Redmond High Desert Trail Map
GPS: 44.3962° N, -120.4258° W
Land Manager: Ochoco National Forest

OVERVIEW

This ride kicks my butt every time, but it is also one of my favorites. You can see that at over 5000 feet of total elevation gain, there is some heavy climbing—you ride up two peaks, no less. There are also some *very* technical downhills off the tops of Round and Lookout mountains. This is truly a ride for only the fittest and most experienced mountain bikers, and it should always be done with a buddy—it's a great all-day ride with friends. Be sure to bring plenty of water and food, tools, and extra clothing; the weather can change dramatically in the Ochoco Mountains, sometimes from sunshine to thunderstorms.

The terrain and ecology of the Ochoco Mountains are quite different than those of the Cascades. You'll find open ponderosa pine forests with native grasses and tons of wildflowers on Round Mountain and the lower portions of Lookout. In late summer and fall, the last brutal section of climbing to the top of Round Mountain winds through false hellebore plants, at times taller than you are. There's also a good chance to see wildlife such as deer, elk, black bears, and wild horses.

GETTING THERE

From the intersection of US Highway 26 (NE 3rd Street) and Main Street in downtown Prineville, take US 26 east. In 16 miles, stay right on Ochoco Creek Road (County Road 23). In another 5 miles, stay right again on Ochoco Ranger Road (CR 23). In 3.2 miles, turn left into the Ochoco Ranger Station and rental cabins. Park here. Across the road you will see the Lookout Mountain Trail, which you will be coming down at the end of the ride.

MILEAGE LOG

0.0 From the Ochoco Ranger Station, take Ochoco Ranger Rd. (CR 23) east.

0.1 Stay left onto paved FR 22. You'll take this road for the next 6.9 miles.

7.0 Just past the intersection with the Walton Lake turnoff, take dirt FR 148 to the Round Mountain North trailhead.

7.2 Get on the Round Mountain Trail and start climbing immediately. Watch for horseback riders and hikers along this section.

10.3 You'll encounter some very steep, very tight switchbacks that lead to the top of Round Mountain.

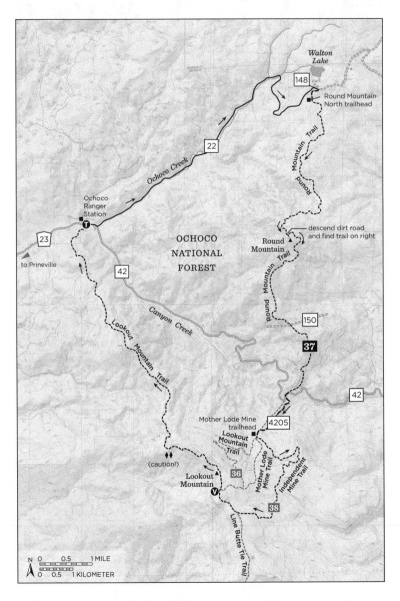

Walton Lake

148

Round Mountain
North trailhead

22

Ochoco Creek

Round Mountain Trail

Ochoco
Ranger
Station

T

23

to Prineville

42

OCHOCO
NATIONAL
FOREST

Round
Mountain ▲

descend dirt road
and find trail on right

Round Mountain Trail

Canyon Creek

150

37

42

Lookout Mountain Trail

Mother Lode Mine
trailhead

4205

Lookout
Mountain
Trail

(caution!)

36

Mother Lode Mine Trail

Independent Mine Trail

Lookout
Mountain
V

38

Line Butte Tie Trail

N 0   0.5   1 MILE
   0   0.5   1 KILOMETER

False hellebore lines the trail on Round Mountain.

11.2 From the summit of Round Mountain, you will take the dirt access road down about a quarter mile to the first turn in the road. Look for the trail that takes off from there, on your right. It is signed.

11.4 Get back on the Round Mountain Trail. This section is rocky and steep.

13.9 Cross dirt FR 150.

16.3 Cross paved FR 42. On the other side, take dirt FR 4205 toward the Mother Lode Mine trailhead.

17.3 At the Mother Lode Mine trailhead, get on the trail to the far left—the Independent Mine Trail. It is the longest but least steep of the three trails that start here. The trail to the far right is the Lookout Mountain Trail and is another good option. The middle trail, the Mother Lode Mine Trail, is very steep and not recommended.

20.8 The Line Butte Tie Trail takes off to the left. Stay straight to continue up Lookout Mountain. The terrain opens up to sagebrush without trees right around here, and the trail gets rocky and a bit steeper in places.

21.3 You're at the Lookout Mountain summit. It's a long, open plateau, so enjoy the big views. When you are ready, head north on the Lookout Mountain Trail to ride the length of the plateau.

21.7 Watch for a very gnarly technical descent with pedal-crushing rocks and super steep switchbacks here! Walking your bike is a good option, especially if you are tired.

22.7 The trail mellows a bit for a fun, rolling descent all the way back to your car. *Warning: There are three uphills along this section, which will catch you by surprise when your legs are cooked from this big ride.*

28.7 Return to the Ochoco Ranger Station, where you parked.

38 INDEPENDENT MINE

LOOP

Trail Type: 100% singletrack
Distance: 8.7 miles
Elevation Gain/Loss: 1750/1750 feet
High Point: 6918 feet
Ride Time: 1–3 hours
Technical Difficulty: Intermediate
Fitness Intensity: Moderate

Season: July–October
Map: Adventure Maps, Sisters & Redmond High Desert Trail Map
GPS: 44.3314° N, -120.3488° W
Land Manager: Ochoco National Forest

OVERVIEW

The Independent Mine loop is a fun loop that includes historic mine buildings, mixed fir forests, tiny creek crossings, stellar views from Lookout Mountain, and, if you hit it right, some great wildflowers. At 8.7 miles and 1750 feet of elevation gain, it's also a steep climb to Lookout Mountain.

The mines are abandoned mercury mines that were first acquired in 1930 and shut down in the 1950s. The route takes the Independent Mine Trail up to Lookout Mountain and then descends the Lookout Mountain Trail. As with most trails in the Ochoco Mountains, watch for equestrians and hikers

A late-season ride, complete with a dusting of snow, on the Independent Mine loop
(Photo: Travis Holman)

on this loop. If you want to learn about the mining history of the area, take a side trip on the quarter-mile Baneberry Loop Interpretive Trail to see the historic buildings along with some nice scenery.

GETTING THERE

From the intersection of US Highway 26 (NE 3rd Street) and Main Street in downtown Prineville, take US 26 east. In 16 miles, stay right on Ochoco Creek Road (County Road 23). In another 5 miles, stay right again on Ochoco Ranger Road (CR 23). In another 3.3 miles, turn right on Forest Road 42 and take this for another 7.2 miles, then turn right on FR 4205. I recommend parking here at the Upper Lookout Mountain trailhead and riding your bike up FR 4205 for a mile to the next trailhead, the Mother Lode Mine trailhead. The road is quite rough and rocky. This way, you also get a little more distance for this loop. Alternatively, you can drive up the road and do the loop from there.

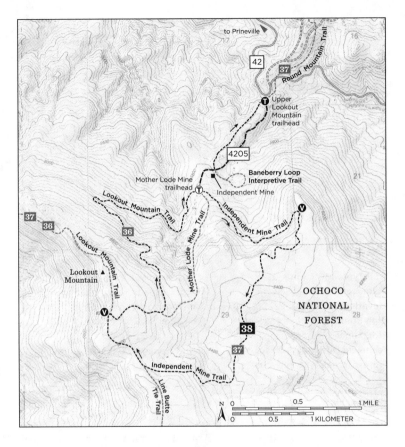

MILEAGE LOG

0.0 Start at the Upper Lookout Mountain trailhead, at the bottom of FR 4205. Ride up FR 4205. It is fairly steep and rocky.

0.9 Here, you've reached the Mother Lode Mine trailhead, an alternative parking area that is popular with hikers. Take the Independent Mine Trail to the left.

1.8 Enjoy the nice views from here.

4.4 The Line Butte Tie Trail goes to the left here. Stay on the main trail to climb up to Lookout Mountain.

4.9 The Lookout Mountain summit is a wide plateau with sweeping views of the Ochocos and Cascade mountains. From here, take the Lookout Mountain Trail to the right.

5.5 Take a left at the intersection with the Mother Lode Mine Trail to stay on the Lookout Mountain Trail.

7.7 At the Mother Lode Mine trailhead, take FR 4205 to where an unnamed trail breaks off to the left. Take this trail, which parallels FR 4205, back to your car. *Option: Stay on FR 4205.*

8.7 Return to where you parked at the Upper Lookout Mountain trailhead at the bottom of FR 4205.

39 COUGAR CREEK

OUT-AND-BACK

Trail Type: 100% singletrack
Distance: 15.8 miles
Elevation Gain/Loss: 2270/2270 feet
High Point: 4888 feet
Ride Time: 3–4 hours
Technical Difficulty: Advanced
Fitness Intensity: Strenuous

Season: June–October
Map: Online at www.fs.usda.gov /recmain/ochoco/recreation (click on the "Cougar East Trailhead" link)
GPS: 44.5253° N, -120.3715° W
Land Manager: Ochoco National Forest

OVERVIEW

The Cougar Creek Trail has just recently been revitalized into a mountain biking trail. According to the Forest Service, this trail is a reconstruction of a historic pack trail that was used from 1915 to 1922. Volunteers with the Crook County Chapter of COTA have been clearing and improving it, and it's been getting more mountain bike use. However, in 2014, the Bailey Butte Fire scorched part of the route, so falling trees are now a big hazard. Definitely don't ride here when it is windy; and even on a calm day, take care.

There are a few ways to ride this trail, but I've written it up here as an out-and-back starting and ending at the Cougar Creek Trailhead East, which is located right off US Highway 26. To reach the other end of the trail, at the Cougar Creek Trailhead West, it is about a 9-mile drive on dirt and gravel roads.

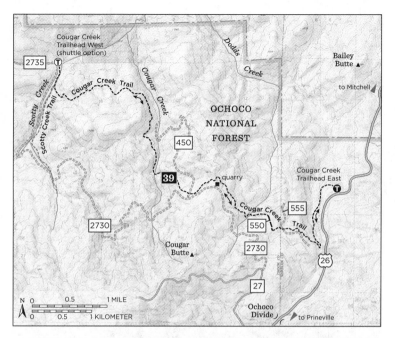

This trail is quite challenging, with significant elevation gain. It's also narrow and rocky in places. Check with Good Bike Co. in Prineville for the most current trail conditions. Note that you can also ride this as a one-way shuttle if you are willing to drive to the far end of the trail to leave a car.

GETTING THERE

From the intersection of US Highway 26 (NE 3rd Street) and Main Street in downtown Prineville, take US 26 East. Drive east 33 miles on US 26 until you reach the Cougar Creek Trailhead East on your left. Park here.

MILEAGE LOG

0.0   Start at the Cougar Creek Trailhead East. For the first mile, the Cougar Creek Trail will contour around the hillside, roughly parallel to the highway.

1.1   Start climbing here.

The Cougar Creek Trail is a revitalized historic pack trail from the early 1900s.
(Photo: Travis Holman)

1.8   Cross FR 555.

2.0   The trail follows FR 550 for 0.2 mile.

2.5   Cross Dodds Creek.

3.4   Reach the quarry. This is the highest point on your ride. From here, you'll descend all the way to the Cougar Creek Trailhead West.

3.9   Cross FR 450.

4.6   Cross Cougar Creek.

7.3   Heads up on the tight switchbacks.

7.9   Reach the Cougar Creek Trailhead West. If you are doing a one-way shuttle, this is where you'd park your second car. Otherwise, turn around and prepare for a 4.5-mile climb back up to the quarry.

8.5   Ride back up those switchbacks!

11.2   Cross Cougar Creek again. This is a great place for a quick break before tackling the steepest pitch of the climb.

11.9   Cross FR 450. The climb mellows out a little bit before reaching the quarry.

12.4   You are now back at the quarry. Continue on the trail and remember that much of it is downhill, with a few short climbs.

13.3   Cross Dodds Creek.

13.8   Ride on FR 550 for a short bit before getting back on the trail.

15.8   End the ride back at the Cougar Creek Trailhead East, where you started.

SISTERS

About 20 miles northwest of Bend, the charming Western-style town of Sisters—popular with cone-lickers (an affectionate term for ice cream–eating tourists)—has a good selection of trails open from early April to late October. If you are traveling en route from the McKenzie River area or the Willamette Valley, this is a nice place to stop for a spin. Some of these routes have excellent views of the Sisters peaks as well as Mount Washington, Mount Jefferson, and Black Butte.

The Central Oregon Trail Alliance (COTA) and the Sisters Trails Alliance (STA) collaborate to maintain the trails here. The STA stewards the Peterson Ridge network of trails (Route 40), and COTA largely maintains the Cache Mountain trails and Trail 99 (Routes 41 and 42). Rumor has it that Black Butte, the symmetrical cone-shaped butte near Camp Sherman, will eventually have mountain-bike-specific trails, so stay tuned for future updates. Blazin Saddles bike shop in Sisters has the latest information on trail conditions.

Sisters is famous for its summertime festivals, the annual Sisters Outdoor Quilt Show, the Sisters Folk Festival, and the Sisters Rodeo—yeehaw! Town can get crowded during those times, but the trails are often empty, so go ride!

40 PETERSON RIDGE

NETWORK

Trail Type: 100% singletrack
Distance: Up to 25 miles
Elevation Gain/Loss: 1160/1160 feet
High Point: 3839 feet

Ride Time: 1–4 hours
Technical Difficulty: Intermediate–advanced
Fitness Intensity: Moderate

Opposite: *A seasoned mountain biker opens it up on the Cache Mountain descent.*

The Three Sisters look close enough to touch from Peterson Ridge.
(Photo: Heidi Faller)

Season: April–November
Map: Adventure Maps, Sisters &
Redmond High Desert Trail Map

GPS: 44.2843° N, -121.5497° W
Land Manager: Deschutes National
Forest

OVERVIEW

The Peterson Ridge Trail (locally known as PRT) network is an awesome network of trails, accessed immediately from Sisters, that was built out over the last decade. Historically these were hiking and horseback riding trails. But as mountain biking gained popularity, the network was improved and expanded into what is now largely a mountain biking area. Still, because the trailhead starts right in the town of Sisters, there are many hikers, dog walkers, and

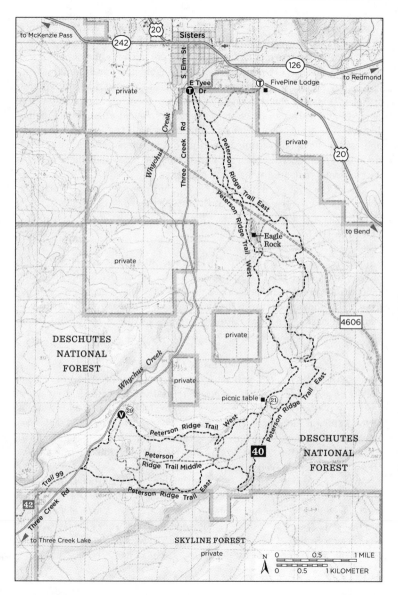

runners who share the trail. The Peterson Ridge Rumble is a trail running race that happens every year in April, so steer clear of the area on race day.

The trails here are much like the Phil's Trail network just outside Bend. They wind through dry ponderosa and lodgepole pine forest, and just like Phil's, they get dusty by early summer. The best times to ride are in March or April. This zone can also get quite muddy in the winter and early spring: heed all mud warnings and stay off the trails to avoid causing long-lasting damage. The trails vary from fast and smooth on the lower sections to tight and technical on the upper sections of the Peterson Ridge Trail West. Hence, the technical difficulty is rated as intermediate to advanced because the trails vary in degree of technical challenge.

One of the coolest things about these trails are the views of North and Middle Sister—so close it seems you can touch them on a clear day.

GETTING THERE

From Bend, head northwest on US Highway 20 to the town of Sisters. In Sisters, turn left on South Elm Street and drive south. In 0.5 mile, look for a small trailhead and parking area on the left at Tyee Drive. Park here. Alternatives: If this spot is too crowded and you can't find a place to park, go back into Sisters and park at the Village Green City Park, which is on South Elm Street. You can also access these trails from FivePine Lodge.

MILEAGE LOG

Because there are more than thirty intersections (most of which are actually signed on the trails, making for easier routefinding), instead of including a play-by-play description, I've left the route open to rider's choice. Think of the Peterson Ridge trails as a curved ladder, with two main trails as the sides—Peterson Ridge Trail East and Peterson Ridge Trail West—and numerous shorter trails, the "rungs," running between them. You can ride a quick one-hour loop or hit every trail on the map.

My favorite way to ride the PRT is to climb up the east trail all the way to Three Creek Rd., then come down the west trail. Be sure to stop at the big rock outcropping viewpoint at intersection 29 and take a look at North and Middle Sister. The PRT West is a fun downhill and quite rocky in places. Right around intersection 21, look for a picnic table just west of the trail. It might be one of the most scenic trailside lunch spots in all of central Oregon.

OPTIONS

You can connect rides in this network to Trail 99 (see Route 42) at the upper (southern) end of the Peterson Ridge system.

41 CACHE MOUNTAIN

LOOP

Trail Type: 50% singletrack, 50% dirt road

Distance: 12 miles

Elevation Gain/Loss: 2190/2190 feet

High Point: 5576 feet

Ride Time: 2–4 hours

Technical Difficulty: Advanced

Fitness Intensity: Strenuous

Season: July–October

Map: Adventure Maps, Sisters & Redmond High Desert Trail Map

GPS: 44.4101° N, -121.7447° W

Land Manager: Deschutes National Forest

OVERVIEW

The Cache Mountain trails have been around for a long time, but it has only been in recent years that they have been revived and maintained for the long haul. In 2003, much of the mountain was burned in the big B&B Complex Fire. As a result, the ceanothus shrubs (known as snowbrush) came back with a vengeance, and it's been tough to keep the trails clear. In the past, this network of trails was cleared each year right before the Big Fat Tour in October, but they remained overgrown and full of downed trees until then. The Big Fat Tour, a weekend of organized big rides, no longer exists. But with an active COTA chapter in Sisters, hopefully these trails will stick around, because they are a scream of a downhill—essentially a bobsled run in loose volcanic soils. Don't ride the trails when it is really windy as there is a very real danger of burnt snags falling. I rode up here once just after a windstorm to be surprised by trees down across the trail around several blind corners.

Routefinding is a challenge on this ride. There are many unnamed trails crisscrossing the lower lakes and a lot of unsigned dirt roads on the way up. The ride described here is not actually mapped out on the Adventure Map, though that is still the best resource for finding your way. Bring a second map to get a good sense of where you are. Also, be prepared to hike-a-bike quite a

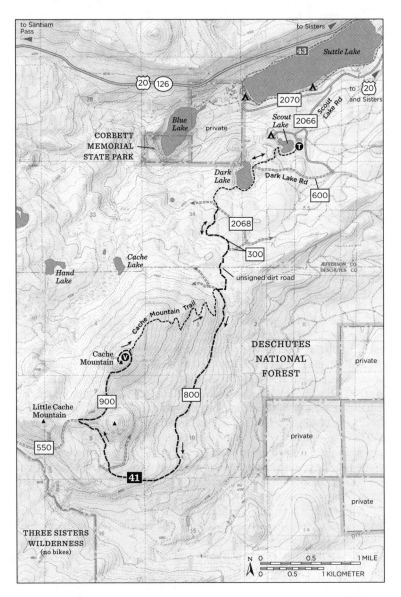

Cache Mountain burned in 2003, but the trails have been revived for mountain biking in the last few years.

bit uphill in the loose pumice tread, as there are some very steep spots. Just remember, you get to ride down it all. Know, too, that this is a popular motorcycling and four-wheeling area, so there is a good chance you might share the dirt roads with other folks.

GETTING THERE

From Bend, take US Highway 20 West toward Sisters. Continue 13 miles past Sisters to Suttle Lake. Turn left on Suttle Lake Road (Forest Road 2070). In 1.2 miles, turn left at Forest Road 2066 to Scout and Dark lakes. When you get to Scout Lake, park on the left-hand side of the road, across from the steps heading down to the lake.

MILEAGE LOG

0.0 Near the top of the steps as you face Scout Lake, take the trail to the left, alongside the lake.

0.3 Take a hard left to continue up the trail, away from Scout Lake.

0.6 Cross Dark Lake Rd. and follow the trail along the south edge of Dark Lake, then grunt up some steep sections.

1.4 At FR 2068, turn left, but watch for the next, very quick, turn.

1.4 At FR 300, turn right.

2.1 Look for an old unsigned dirt road and turn right onto this.

2.6 Turn left on FR 800. You'll stay on this for a while, so get comfortable climbing.

5.3 There will be an intersection with another road to the right that goes off to a peak just ahead. This usually confuses riders. This is *not* Cache Mountain, so stay on the main road (straight). At this point, the road you are on is labeled FR 900 on maps.

6.0 Take the hard right at this intersection.

6.9 Now you are starting to climb and wrap around Cache Mountain. It gets steeper with loose cinders the closer you get to the summit. Look closely to the right and you might see the trail dropping off of the road.

7.3 You're at the top. Good job getting there. Take in the 360-degree view. You'll also notice remnants from an old Forest Service fire lookout. Turn around when you are ready and take the road back down for a short bit.

7.7 The trail to take down—the Cache Mountain Trail—will be on your left. It may be very faint to discourage the motorcycles from using it, so look closely. From here, it's a bobsled run. Watch out for downed and dead trees from the B&B Complex Fire in 2003.

9.4 Cross dirt FR 800 and continue ahead on the unsigned dirt road. You should recognize the way, as you rode up it earlier today. From here, you will retrace your steps to get back to where you started.

9.9 Turn left on FR 300.

10.6 Turn left onto FR 2068. Watch for the trail on the right!

10.6 Take this quick right onto the trail to Dark Lake. Remember those steep sections you hiked up? Now you get to go down them.

11.4 Cross Dark Lake Rd.

11.7 Turn right to go counterclockwise around Scout Lake, back to your parking spot.

12.0 End at the Scout Lake parking area.

The Cache Mountain ride delivers awesome views of nearby Cascade peaks while contouring through charred forest.

42 TRAIL 99

SHUTTLE

Trail Type: 100% singletrack
Distance: 13.2 miles
Elevation Gain/Loss: 680/3830 feet
High Point: 6390 feet
Ride Time: 3–4 hours
Technical Difficulty: Advanced
Fitness Intensity: Moderate

Season: July–October
Map: Adventure Maps, Sisters & Redmond High Desert Trail Map
GPS: Start: 44.1176° N, -121.6285° W; End: 44.2224° N, -121.5763° W
Land Manager: Deschutes National Forest

OVERVIEW

Trail 99 is also the Metolius–Windigo Trail, but in this area, this section of that trail is known as Trail 99. This is a virtually all-downhill trail, with some steep, technical, rocky descents in the upper stretches. While I've written it up as a shuttle, you can certainly do it as an out-and-back by starting at the bottom and riding up as far as you want before turning around.

Riders start their descent on Trail 99. (Photo: Daisy LaPoma)

Trail 99 starts just below Three Creek Lake. This is a popular horse camping area, so Trail 99 is also a popular horseback riding trail. In fact, in late summer it can see a lot of equestrian use, making it quite sandy in places.

The Pole Creek Fire of 2012 burned much of the forest surrounding the upper region of the trail, leaving the tread exposed to the sun, making it even sandier. There is a high risk of burnt snags falling, so don't ride this on a windy day. The good news about the burn is that you get some nice views of the Three Sisters. Check with Blazin Saddles bike shop in Sisters for the latest trail conditions.

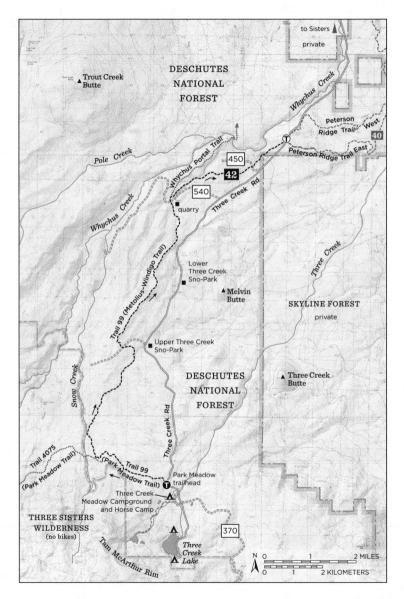

GETTING THERE

To reach the start of the ride at the Park Meadow trailhead: From Bend, head northwest on US Highway 20 to the town of Sisters. In Sisters, turn left on South Elm Street and drive south. South Elm Street turns into Three Creek Road. Drive south 14.3 miles to the Park Meadow trailhead, an open gravel parking lot on the left, and park here. The trail takes off on the other side of the road, just up from the parking area.

To reach the end of the ride: From Bend, drive to Sisters. Turn left on South Elm Street and drive south (it turns into Three Creek Road). In 5.3 miles, you will reach the spot where the Peterson Ridge trails head to the left and Trail 99 heads to the right. There is a small gravel parking area here on the right.

MILEAGE LOG

0.0 From the Park Meadow trailhead, cross the road to get on Trail 99 (Park Meadow Trail). There is a short climb at the very beginning.

2.2 At the intersection where Trail 4075 (Park Meadow Trail) heads west, turn right to stay on Trail 99. You will be skirting the Three Sisters Wilderness, which is closed to bicycles.

5.3 Cross an unsigned snowmobile road. Stay on Trail 99.

7.6 Hang on for some steeper, rockier sections through here.

9.8 Immediately at the quarry, cross dirt FR 540.

9.9 Right after crossing the dirt road, you'll see the Whychus Portal Trail to the left. This is a hiker-only trail. Stay on Trail 99, which will use an old dirt road for portions of this section.

12.1 Cross FR 450.

13.2 This is the end of Trail 99. If you parked here, you are done.

OPTIONS

To add more onto this ride, continue on the Peterson Ridge trails all the way to Sisters (see Route 40). For this option, leave your second car at the main Peterson Ridge trailhead.

43 SUTTLE TIE TO SUTTLE LAKE

OUT-AND-BACK

Trail Type: 100% singletrack
Distance: 13.7 miles
Elevation Gain/Loss: 650/650 feet
High Point: 3469 feet
Ride Time: 1–2 hours
Technical Difficulty: Beginner
Fitness Intensity: Easy

Season: April–October
Map: Adventure Maps, Sisters & Redmond High Desert Trail Map
GPS: 44.3925° N, -121.6744° W
Land Manager: Deschutes National Forest

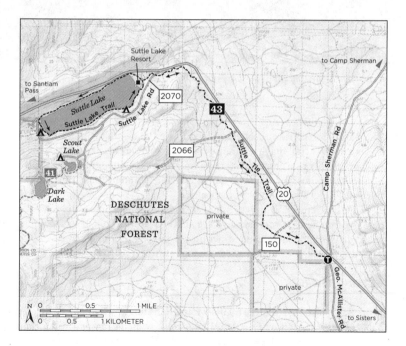

Suttle Lake is another gorgeous lake in the Cascades.

OVERVIEW

The Suttle Tie Trail connects the Black Butte Ranch area with Suttle Lake and is a mellow trail that uses a series of old singletrack and old roads. This is a superb family ride or a good starting trail for the beginner mountain biker. Most of the trail is smooth and fairly wide. There are some rocks and roots on the Suttle Lake Trail, but they are minimal.

The trail starts in dry ponderosa and lodgepole pine forest, which changes into mixed fir forest as you reach the lake. Suttle Lake is a popular summertime hangout with good swimming and boating opportunities, so on a hot day it makes for a good midday hangout.

GETTING THERE

From Bend, take US Highway 20 West toward the town of Sisters. At 9.6 miles past Sisters, turn left on Geo. McAllister Road, which is across from Camp Sherman Road. You will see the Suttle Tie Trail immediately. Park here.

MILEAGE LOG

0.0 Start on the Suttle Tie Trail and ride northwest.

0.9 Cross dirt FR 150, staying on the trail.

1.6 Here, the trail uses a series of old forest roads, so follow the signs to stay on the route.

2.7 Cross dirt FR 2066.

4.9 After a steeper climb, you'll reach the Suttle Lake Resort area. Look for the Suttle Lake Trail to the right to proceed around the lake in a counterclockwise direction.

6.6 At the far west end of the lake, you'll ride through campgrounds, day-use areas, and boat ramp access points. Continue around the lake on the Suttle Lake Trail.

8.8 Near the resort, turn right onto the Suttle Tie Trail to ride back to where you started.

11.0 Cross FR 2066.

12.8 Cross FR 150.

13.7 Return to your parked car at Geo. McAllister Rd.

McKENZIE RIVER

Although it is only a two-hour drive from Bend, the McKenzie River valley is a complete contrast to central Oregon. Located on the other side of Santiam Pass in the western Cascades, this area oozes with lush old-growth forests dripping with vibrant green moss, giant ferns, and the cold, clear waters of the McKenzie River and its tributaries. I may be biased, but I think the McKenzie River is one of the most beautiful rivers in Oregon. This region is truly a magical place, worthy of a mountain bike bucket list.

The trails here are not for the beginner rider because they are rocky, rooty, twisty, and steep, and they often wind along a steep embankment or cliff. It also rains more frequently here, making the trails even more challenging as those roots become slicker than snot. And even if it has not rained, the trails can remain damp for days on end in the dark forest. Be prepared to up your game on these trails.

All services such as food, drink, gas, and lodging are found along the McKenzie River Highway (Oregon Route 126). Blazin Saddles opened up a small bike shop here, and Horse Creek Lodge offers mountain-bike-friendly accommodations near the McKenzie River Trail and the King Castle and Olallie/O'Leary networks. The lodge rents rooms and cabins and has an outdoor fire pit and a pump track, among other amenities. Camping is also available at numerous Forest Service campgrounds in the area, which all require a camping fee.

Opposite: *A rider welcomes a short, flat stretch on the mostly steep, uphill Olallie Trail.*

44 McKENZIE RIVER TRAIL

SHUTTLE

Trail Type: 100% singletrack
Distance: 24.9 miles
Elevation Gain/Loss: 860/2580 feet
High Point: 3152 feet
Ride Time: 4–6 hours
Technical Difficulty: Advanced
Fitness Intensity: Strenuous

Season: April–October
Map: Adventure Maps, Sisters &
Redmond High Desert Trail Map
GPS: Start: 44.3944° N, -122.0021° W;
End: 44.1770° N, -122.1364° W
Land Manager: Willamette National
Forest

OVERVIEW

The McKenzie River Trail (MRT) is an incredible trail, and is unlike any other mountain bike trail in the area and perhaps in all of Oregon. *Bike Magazine* and *Men's Fitness* both declared the MRT the number one mountain biking trail in America. You'll see giant granddaddy trees, hanging gardens of moss, and waterfalls, and you'll experience numerous log creek crossings, hot springs, and the infamous Blue Pool. In September and October, when the maple trees and vine maple bushes turn color to lose their leaves, you can catch a spectacular fall display.

This ride can be done as an out-and-back or as a one-way shuttle; I recommend the shuttle to get the full experience. However, do not think for one moment that this is a downhill forest cruise! Even though your net elevation loss will be around 1700 feet, this is a challenging and strenuous ride as the trail goes continuously up and down, up and down. It is also very technical in places, particularly for the upper half, from Clear Lake to Trail Bridge Reservoir. There are some extremely tough sections of sharp lava rock through which all but the most skilled riders hike. Even though the trail follows the river, which roughly follows the highway, it is still quite remote and there are few access points, so be prepared to take care of yourself for the long haul.

If you choose to embark on a shorter ride, you can always park at the lower trailhead and ride up the trail as far as you like, then turn around and head back. The lower half of the trail is less challenging than the upper half. There are several commercial shuttle operators for this trail, including Bend-based Cog Wild Mountain Bike Tours and, in the McKenzie River valley, Horse

A rough and rowdy section of the McKenzie River Trail (Photo: Melanie Fisher)

Creek Lodge (see Resources, Guides and Shuttle Services). The MRT is a highly popular hiking trail, especially on the weekends, so make your presence known and be courteous to all trail users. The Forest Service has plans to reroute portions of the trail for mountain bikers to avoid biker-hiker conflicts in the future.

GETTING THERE

To reach the start of the ride at the Upper McKenzie River trailhead: From Bend, take US Highway 20 West toward Santiam Pass, about 40 to 50 miles depending on where you start in Bend. At 4.5 miles past Hoodoo Ski Area, stay left on US 20. In another 3.4 miles, stay left on Oregon Route 126 toward Eugene. In 2 miles, look for a sign for the McKenzie River Trail to your left, just past Fish Lake. Turn left here and park.

To reach the end of the ride at the Lower McKenzie River trailhead, near the small community of McKenzie Bridge: Continue on OR 126 past the upper trailhead, described above, for another 21 miles. About a mile past the ranger station on your left, you'll come to the Lower McKenzie River

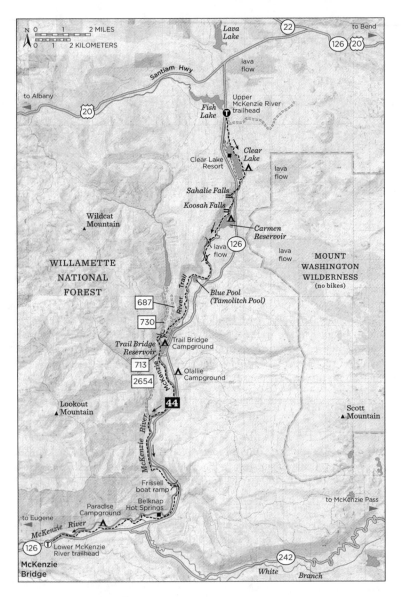

trailhead. If you are organizing your own shuttle, this is where you will park your second vehicle.

MILEAGE LOG

0.0 At the Upper McKenzie River trailhead, just across the road from Fish Lake, get on the MRT to ride south.

0.9 At Clear Lake, you can ride on either side of the lake. Take the trail to the left, on the lake's east side, which is more challenging than the trail hugging it on the west side.

2.7 The two trails rejoin just south of the lake; continue south on the MRT.

2.9 Be careful crossing OR 126!

4.0 Sahalie Falls is the first big waterfall that you'll see. In the spring, a large volume of water thunders through here.

5.0 Carmen Reservoir marks the beginning of what locals call the "lava section." For the next few miles, you'll ride adjacent to and through a lava flow with razor-sharp rocks. Aren't you glad you brought that extra tube and patch kit? Be careful through this section and remember, there is no shame in walking.

8.5 You're at Blue Pool (also known as Tamolitch Pool), and you'll know when you are there because you'll come across the most impossibly clear, topaz-colored pool. Intrepid riders and hikers have jumped into this pool, only to discover that they end up in very, very cold water. I don't recommend it. It's a dangerous jump with a long way down into that cold water. Also, watch for hikers here.

10.6 Cross FR 687.

11.6 Cross FR 730. This road takes you to Trail Bridge Reservoir if you need a bailout point. There are two roads that cross the water over to the highway, one to the north and one to the south. From here, the trail becomes a little easier, but you still need to be on your toes for technical sections and steep climbs.

15.8 Cross FR 2654.

19.2 Cross the McKenzie River at Frissell boat ramp. The trail will be between the highway and the river for the remainder of the ride.

20.7 Cross Belknap Hot Springs Rd. (the developed hot springs will be to your right), and continue on the trail.

23.2 Enter Paradise Campground and continue west on the trail.

24.9 Reach the Lower McKenzie River trailhead for the end of the ride.

45 KING CASTLE TO CASTLE ROCK

OUT-AND-BACK

Trail Type: 90% singletrack, 10% dirt road
Distance: 13.2 miles
Elevation Gain/Loss: 3000/3000 feet
High Point: 3780 feet
Ride Time: 2–3 hours
Technical Difficulty: Advanced

Fitness Intensity: Strenuous
Season: July–October
Map: Adventure Maps, Sisters & Redmond High Desert Trail Map
GPS: 44.1730° N, -122.2210° W
Land Manager: Willamette National Forest

OVERVIEW

This out-and-back proves that you don't need a lot of mileage to get in a good workout, as this is definitely one of those "go up then go down" kind of rides. You'll climb 3000 feet in less than 7 miles, so it's a steep one. Enjoy some nice scenery along the way, including big, old trees and wide, open slopes. From the top of Castle Rock, you can look down into the McKenzie River valley and up the steep, forested hillsides of the western Cascades. As you do for all mountain rides, be sure to check the weather before you go. Summer thunderstorms can ruin a good ride and prevent you from getting to the top. I've written this route starting from the gas station in Rainbow because it gives you a little warm-up on pavement before having to climb immediately once on the trail.

Note that trail crews have been rerouting some sections of these trails, so portions of the route may be different than what is described.

GETTING THERE

From Bend, take US Highway 20 West toward Santiam Pass, about 40 to 50 miles depending on where you start in Bend. At 4.5 miles past Hoodoo Ski Area, stay left on US 20. In another 3.4 miles, stay left on Oregon Route 126 toward Eugene. Continue for another 27.4 miles until you reach the

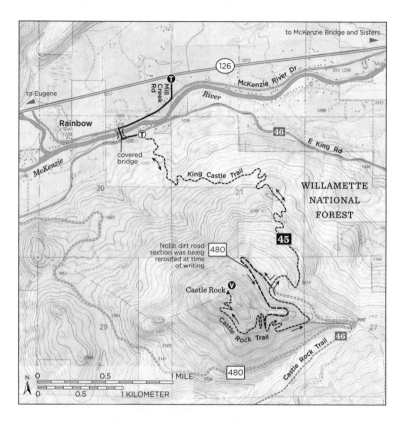

community of Rainbow, just past the Tokatee Golf Course on the right. You'll see a gas station (currently a Shell station), a mini-mart, and a restaurant on your left; park here, in the lot behind the gas station.

MILEAGE LOG

0.0   From the gas station, turn right (head south) on Mill Creek Rd.

0.1   Turn right on McKenzie River Dr.

0.6   Turn left to cross the river through the covered bridge.

0.7   Turn left on E. King Rd.

0.9 Turn right into the King Castle trailhead and hop on the King Castle Trail. You will start climbing right away, encountering switchbacks within the next mile.

4.6 Turn right onto dirt FR 480. You have the option to remain on the trail (you'll see it to the left); however, it is extremely steep. Most riders take the dirt road for a mellower climb. Don't worry, you'll be returning along the singletrack the whole way. *Note: At the time of writing, trail builders were working on rerouting a portion of the route to bypass part of this dirt road, which may make it more enjoyable to ride up the trail, rather than the road. Pay attention to new trails or reroutes.*

The King Castle downhill is fast and fun, winding through old-growth forest.

5.5 Reach Castle Rock Trail and turn right to reach the summit of Castle Rock. The trail gets very steep, especially near the top. Many riders leave their bikes somewhere up here to finish this part as a hike, without a bike.

6.5 You're at the top of Castle Rock. Good job! After you get your fill of views, head back down the trail.

8.1 Pay close attention to find this next intersection. Turn left to drop back down on King Castle Trail.

8.6 Cross FR 480. From here, enjoy a fast and furious downhill to the trailhead. *Again, this area was being rerouted at the time of writing, so things may look different.*

12.3 From the trailhead, turn left onto E. King Rd.

12.5 Turn right to cross the river through the covered bridge.

12.6 Turn right on McKenzie River Dr.

13.1 Turn left on Mill Creek Rd.

13.2 Return to where you parked your car and started the ride at the gas station.

46 OLALLIE AND O'LEARY EPIC

LOOP

Trail Type: 70% singletrack, 30% pavement

Distance: 27.8 miles

Elevation Gain/Loss: 5700/5700 feet

High Point: 5105 feet

Ride Time: 5–8 hours

Technical Difficulty: Expert

Fitness Intensity: Very strenuous

Season: July–October; check with the McKenzie River Ranger District for trail status

Map: Adventure Maps, Sisters & Redmond High Desert Trail Map

GPS: 44.1730° N, -122.2210° W

Land Manager: Willamette National Forest

OVERVIEW

I've saved the best for last. The first time I rode this loop, in 2004, I rode it partially, and then I returned to ride the full route in 2009. Back then the trails had not been cleared or maintained, and long sections were totally blocked with berry bushes and downed trees. It took, literally, all day to ride, push, and hike—up and down. Since then, volunteer crews with the Central Oregon Trail Alliance (COTA), Disciples of Dirt (DOD), and Greater Oakridge Area Trail Stewards (GOATS) have worked hard to keep these trails open and improved, which is totally awesome for this epic ride.

Riding the route again in 2015 while researching this book, I was still quite humbled by its toughness. It is a truly epic western Cascades mountain bike loop and should only be attempted by advanced to expert riders. It is remote and challenging and includes hiking your bike, both up and down, for significant sections. The routefinding is often tricky; you'll need all your skills about you. It is advised that you don't do this ride alone. Bring a strong group of mountain biker buddies with you, and have adequate food, water, and supplies to get you through the day.

If you can muster up the gumption for this ride, you'll experience the rugged solitude of the western Oregon Cascades with old-growth forests, wildflower-laden meadows, historic trails built by the Civilian Conservation Corps, and the potential for loads of wildlife. There are a few options for the ride. Of them, the write-up below is the most demanding with the longest amount of singletrack. But you can ride the road or shuttle to the top of the Olallie Trail to tone it down a bit. As of this writing, FR 1993 was impassable between the Olallie trailhead and FR 340 due to a large landslide. If you want to drive to the upper part of the Olallie Trail, at the point where it crosses FR 340, you'll need to consult the Adventure Map or a Willamette National Forest map to find an alternate route.

Note that trail crews have been rerouting some sections of these trails, so portions of the route may be different than what is described.

GETTING THERE

From Bend, take US Highway 20 West toward Santiam Pass, about 40 to 50 miles depending on where you start in Bend. At 4.5 miles past Hoodoo Ski Area, stay left on US 20. In another 3.4 miles, stay left on Oregon Route 126 toward Eugene. Continue for another 27.4 miles until you reach the community of Rainbow, just past the Tokatee Golf Course on the right. You'll see a gas station (currently a Shell station), a mini-mart, and a restaurant on your left; park here, in the lot behind the gas station. Load up on food here, too. You'll need it!

MILEAGE LOG

0.0   From the gas station, turn right (head south) on Mill Creek Rd.

0.1   Turn right on McKenzie River Dr.

0.6   Turn left to cross the river through the covered bridge.

0.7   Turn left on E. King Rd. and follow this paved road for over 4 miles.

5.0   Turn right on Horse Creek Rd.

5.3   Pass Horse Creek Campground.

5.4   Turn right on FR 1993. Climb this quiet, paved road for about 3 miles. The road has short gravel sections.

8.3   You've reached the Olallie trailhead. Get ready to climb narrow single-track for the next 4 miles. There are really no breaks, just steady

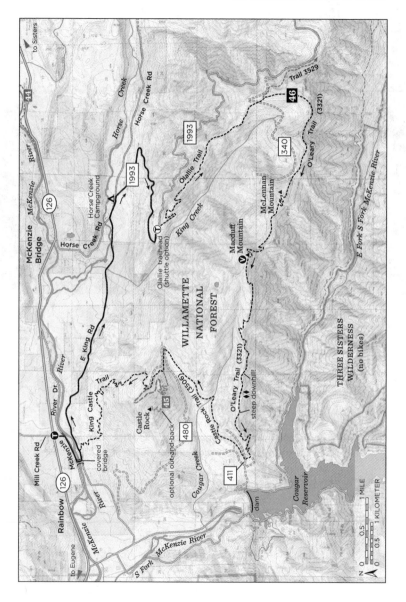

The remote O'Leary Trail, seen from Macduff Mountain
(Photo: Chris Kratsch)

climbing. The Olallie Trail is very narrow with steep drop-offs, so be really careful. It's also gorgeous—this is some of the most beautiful forest you can ride through.

11.4 Cross FR 340.

11.5 This is the intersection with Trail 3529 and O'Leary Trail (Trail 3321). Turn right onto O'Leary Trail. The first few miles of this beautiful trail are through meadows and along open ridges. There are sections that are often overgrown with vegetation, so watch for hidden obstacles and holes in the trail.

13.1 The trail becomes less flat and more rolling as you pass by McLennan Mountain and head on toward Macduff Mountain. There are some steep, unrideable switchbacks that you'll have to hike, as well as rocky terrain.

15.6 You've arrived at Macduff Mountain. You'll know because the trail goes through a more open, drier section. The summit is a short scramble up to the top of the ridge to your right. Take the time to hike up there—the views of the western Oregon Cascades and the McKenzie River valley are definitely worth it! After Macduff Mountain, prepare for a long, challenging downhill.

18.6 At this point on the downhill, the trail follows a very steep ridgeline with some improbably hairball switchbacks. It will look like you are falling off the edge of the earth. Unless you are a pro downhiller, you might want to get off your bike and walk. It's a long section. *Note: As of this writing, trail volunteer groups were building new, more rideable sections of trail in this area, so expect to see changes in the future.*

19.7 At the bottom of the steep downhill, cross FR 411.

19.8 Turn right on Castle Rock Trail (Trail 3506) for some more climbing (but not as brutal as what you've already done). This is a critical intersection to watch for, because if you take the wrong trail, you will end up on the other side of the ridge, very far from where you want to be.

22.4 Cross FR 480 and continue on the Castle Rock Trail.

22.7 Stay to the right on King Castle Trail for a really fun downhill to the King Castle trailhead. You deserve it. *Option: There's an opportunity here to bag another peak if you have some juice left. For the 1.6-mile climb up to Castle Rock, take a left here (see Route 45). It's steep.*

26.9 At the King Castle trailhead, turn left on E. King Rd.

27.1 Turn right to cross the river through the covered bridge.

27.2 Turn right on McKenzie River Dr.

27.7 Turn left on Mill Creek Rd.

27.8 Return to your car at the gas station. Enjoy a cold beverage and a corn dog at the mini-mart before driving home after this epic ride!

RESOURCES

GUIDES AND SHUTTLE SERVICES

While this book will hopefully inspire you to explore Bend's mountain bike trails on your own, sometimes having a professional guide can enhance the experience. Below are guides and shuttle services available for the trails listed in this book.

Based in Bend, **Cog Wild Mountain Bike Tours** organizes guided day and multiday mountain bike trips in the Deschutes, Willamette, and Ochoco national forests for riders of all levels. Their guides are very experienced, knowledgeable, and a whole lot of fun. Cog Wild also offers McKenzie River Trail shuttles.

    255 SW Century Drive, Suite 201
    Bend, OR 97702
    866-610-4822 or 541-385-7002
    www.cogwild.com

The bike shop in Prineville, **Good Bike Co.**, offers singletrack and dirt road mountain bike tours in the Ochoco National Forest.

    541-903-0509
    www.goodbikeco.com

The **Paulina Plunge** is a special ride that can be accessed only with the Paulina Plunge outfitter, based in La Pine. This guided, family-friendly mountain bike day trip starts at the Newberry Caldera rim and descends dirt roads and singletrack paralleling Paulina Creek. Along the way, riders stop to swim in the creek and play on natural rock "slides."

    53750 Highway 97
    La Pine, OR 97739
    541-389-0562
    www.paulinaplunge.com

Horse Creek Lodge in McKenzie Bridge offers McKenzie River Trail and Olallie/O'Leary loop shuttles.

    56228 Delta Drive
    McKenzie Bridge, OR 97413
    541-822-3243
    www.horse-creek.com

Opposite: *Riders take a break at a panoramic viewpoint on the Grasslands loop, Route 4.*

Several nationally based bike tour companies have permits to guide in the Deschutes National Forest: **Escape Adventures** (www.escapeadventures .com), **Rim Tours** (www.rimtours.com), and **Trek Travel** (www.trektravel.com).

BIKE SHOPS
Bend
Bend has a solid array of bike shops to serve all types of cyclists. The following shops sell mountain bikes, rent mountain bikes, or offer both options.

Bend Cyclery
133 SW Century Drive, Suite 202
Bend, OR 97702
541-385-5256
www.bendcyclery.com

Bend Velo Bike Shop
1212 NE 1st Street
Bend, OR 97701
541-382-2453
www.bendvelo.com

Crows Feet Commons
875 NW Brooks Street
Bend, OR 97701
541-728-0066
www.crowsfeetcommons.com

Gravity Sports at Mount Bachelor
West Village Lodge at Mount Bachelor
541-382-2442
www.mtbachelor.com

Hutch's Eastside
820 NE 3rd Street
Bend, OR 97701
541-382-6248
www.hutchsbicycles.com

Hutch's Westside
725 NW Columbia Street
Bend, OR 97701

541-382-9253
www.hutchsbicycles.com

MWS Sports
170 Scalehouse Loop
Bend, OR 97702
541-633-7694
www.mountainwatersnow.com

Pine Mountain Sports
255 SW Century Drive
Bend, OR 97702
541-385-8080
www.pinemountainsports.com

Recreational Equipment, Inc. (REI)
380 Powerhouse Drive
Bend, OR 97702
541-385-0594
www.rei.com/stores/bend

Sagebrush Cycles
35 SW Century Drive
Bend, OR 97702
541-389-4224
www.sagebrushcycles.net

Sunnyside Sports
930 NW Newport Avenue
Bend, OR 97703
541-382-8018
www.sunnysidesports.com

The Hub Cyclery
1001 NW Wall Street, Suite 102
Bend, OR 97701
541-647-2614
www.thehubcyclerybend.com

WebCyclery
550 SW Industrial Way, Suite 150
Bend, OR 97702
541-318-6188
www.webcyclery.com

Redmond
Hutch's Redmond
827 SW 7th Street
Redmond, OR 97756
541-548-8200
www.hutchsbicycles.com

Trinity Bikes
865 SW 17th Street, Suite 301
Redmond, OR 97756
541-923-5650
www.trinitybikes.com

Sisters
Blazin Saddles
413 West Hood Avenue
Sisters, OR 97759
541-719-1213
www.blazinsaddleshub.com

Eurosports
223 East Hood Avenue
Sisters, OR 97759
541-549-2471
www.eurosports.us

Sunriver
4 Seasons Recreational Outfitters
57195 Beaver Drive
Sunriver, OR 97707
541-593-2255
www.4sro.com

Sunriver Sports
57100 Mall Drive #16
Sunriver, OR 97707
541-593-8369
www.sunriversports.com

Village Bike and Ski
57100 Beaver Drive
Sunriver, OR 97707
541-593-2453
www.villagebikeandski.com

Prineville
Good Bike Co.
284 NE 3rd Street
Prineville, OR 97754
541-903-0509
www.goodbikeco.com

McKenzie River Valley
Blazin Saddles
54771 McKenzie Highway
Blue River, OR 97413
541-854-2292
www.blazinsaddleshub.com

LAND MANAGERS AND TRAIL ORGANIZATIONS

The routes described in this guidebook are located on lands managed by the following agencies. Below, you will also find contact information for the mountain bike trail stewardship organizations that build and maintain the trails.

Land Managers
Deschutes National Forest
www.fs.usda.gov/main/deschutes/home
Deschutes National Forest supervisor's office and Bend–Fort Rock Ranger District
  63095 Deschutes Market Road
  Bend, OR 97701
  541-383-5300 (supervisor's office)
  541-383-4000 (Bend–Fort Rock office)
  Open year round, Monday–Friday,
    8:00 AM–4:30 PM
Cascade Lakes Welcome Station
  18390 Century Drive
  Bend, OR 97702
  May 1–mid-November, open seven
    days a week, 8:00 AM–4:00 PM; mid-
    November–April 30, open Saturday
    and Sunday only, 8:00 AM–4:00 PM

Crescent Ranger District
136471 Highway 97 North/PO Box 208
Crescent, OR 97733
541-433-3200
Open year round, Monday–Friday,
8:00 AM–4:30 PM

Sisters Ranger District
Pine Street and Highway 20/
PO Box 249
Sisters, OR 97759
541-549-7700
Open year round, Monday–Friday,
8:00 AM–4:30 PM

Lava Lands Visitor Center,
Newberry National Volcanic
Monument
58201 South Highway 97
Bend, OR 97707
541-593-2421
Open May 1–October 31. Call for
specific open hours.

Willamette National Forest
www.fs.usda.gov/willamette/
Willamette National Forest
supervisor's office
3106 Pierce Parkway, Suite D
Springfield, OR 97477
541-225-6300
r6_willamette_wwweb_frontdesk
@fs.fed.us
Open year round, Monday–Friday,
8:00 AM–4:30 PM

McKenzie River Ranger District
57600 McKenzie Highway
McKenzie Bridge, OR 97413
541-822-3381
Open year round, Monday–Friday,
8:00 AM–4:30 PM

Middle Fork Ranger District
46375 Highway 58
Westfir, OR 97492
541-782-2283

Open year round, Monday–Friday,
8:00 AM–4:30 PM

Ochoco National Forest and Crooked
River National Grassland
www.fs.usda.gov/ochoco
Ochoco National Forest supervisor's
office and Lookout Mountain
Ranger District
3160 NE 3rd Street/PO Box 490
Prineville, OR 97754
541-416-6500
Open year round, Monday–Friday,
8:00 AM–4:30 PM

Crooked River National Grassland
office
274 SW 4th Street
Madras, OR 97741
541-416-6640
Open year round, Monday–Friday,
8:00 AM–4:30 PM

Oregon Parks and Recreation
Department
www.oregon.gov/oprd
www.oregonstateparks.org (search for
Smith Rock State Park)
800-551-6949 (for general park
information)
OPRD Salem headquarters
725 Summer Street NE, Suite C
Salem, OR 97301
503-986-0707

Bureau of Land Management,
Prineville District
www.blm.gov/or/districts/prineville/
Prineville District office
3050 NE 3rd Street
Prineville, OR 97754
541-416-6700
BLM_OR_PR_Mail@blm.gov
Open year round, Monday–Friday,
7:45 AM–4:30 PM

**Mount Bachelor ski area
(Mount Bachelor Bike Park)**
www.mtbachelor.com
 Main office
   13000 SW Century Drive
   Bend, OR 97702
   800-829-2442
   info@mtbachelor.com

Bend Park and Recreation District
www.bendparksandrec.org
 BPRD main office
   799 SW Columbia Street
   Bend, OR 97702
   541-389-7275
   info@bendparksandrec.org

**Redmond Area Park and Recreation
District**
www.raprd.org
 RAPRD main office
   465 SW Rimrock Drive
   Redmond, OR 97756
   541-548-7275
   raprd@raprd.org

Trail Organizations
**International Mountain Bicycling
Association (IMBA)**
www.imba.com
 IMBA headquarters
   4888 Pearl East Circle, Suite 200E
   Boulder, CO 80301
 IMBA mailing address
   PO Box 20280
   Boulder, CO 80308

**Central Oregon Trail Alliance
(COTA)**
www.cotamtb.com
   PO Box 555
   Bend, OR 97709

**Greater Oakridge Area Trail
Stewards (GOATS)**
www.oakridgegoats.org
   PO Box 584
   Oakridge, OR 97463

Disciples of Dirt (DOD)
www.disciplesofdirt.org
   PO Box 50213
   Eugene, OR 97405

Sisters Trails Alliance (STA)
www.sisterstrails.org
   PO Box 1871
   Sisters, OR 97759

VISIT CENTRAL OREGON
Each of the regions described in this book have options for lodging, camping, food and drink, and amenities.

Bend, Sunriver, and La Pine
Bend is central Oregon's hub and has many options for lodging, camping, food and drink, and other activities. Lodging can range from VRBO-style vacation rentals and Airbnb options to boutique or chain hotels and motels. Camping near Bend includes designated campgrounds in the Deschutes National Forest as well as dispersed camping in the forest. Check with the Bend–Fort Rock Ranger District of the Deschutes National Forest for details on camping.

Bend has an amazing selection of restaurants that range from economical food carts to fine-dining establishments. Of course, what central Oregon is most famous for is our craft breweries. Some of these breweries have full restaurants, and others, only small taprooms. No matter, they all pour fantastic craft brews. If you're not sure where to start, you can embark on the Bend Ale

Trail, your gateway to beervana, which includes an atlas and passport book, all supplied by Visit Bend.

Sunriver is a community and resort property about 15 miles south of Bend that has many vacation homes and condos as well as a good selection of restaurants. **La Pine** is about 30 miles south of Bend, just west of the Newberry Caldera (Route 34).

www.visitbend.com
www.visitcentraloregon.com
www.sunriverchamber.com
www.lapine.org

Redmond and Terrebonne

Just 15 miles north of Bend, **Redmond** is a smaller community that has recently revitalized its downtown scene with funky pubs and restaurants. Redmond also has a number of hotels, bed and breakfasts, and other lodging options. The primary airport to fly into in central Oregon, Roberts Field, is also located in Redmond. **Terrebonne** is the small community near Smith Rock State Park. It has a small grocery store, a pizza place, and the Terrebonne Depot, which is a superb restaurant housed in an old train depot.

www.visitredmondoregon.com

Sisters

Sisters country includes the towns of Sisters, Camp Sherman, Suttle Lake, and Black Butte, all situated off of US Highway 20, northwest of Bend. These communities are quite small but have good options for food and lodging.

www.sisterscountry.com

Prineville

Prineville is a friendly community with a budding bicycle culture. Prineville has a local brewery, other dining options, and a handful of hotels. Also be sure to visit the Good Bike Co.—they have beer on tap.

www.visitprineville.org

McKenzie River

Amenities in the McKenzie River valley are all situated on or just off the McKenzie River Highway (Oregon Route 126). There are Forest Service campgrounds, cabins for rent, rustic lodges, and a few other services, such as gas stations and a few cafes.

www.visitmckenzieriver.com

Waldo Lake

The rides listed in the Waldo Lake section are routes that are in more remote areas, so there aren't as many services and amenities, other than campgrounds in the Deschutes National Forest and the Willamette National Forest. There are, however, a few lake lodges on Cascade Lakes Scenic Byway and OR 58: Elk Lake Resort, Cultus Lake Resort, Lava Lake Resort, and Crescent Lake Resort. All are rustic mountain lodges with camping and/or cabin options, restaurants, and mini-markets. Twenty miles from the road leading into Waldo Lake is Crescent Lake Junction on OR 58. It has a small market and Manley's Tavern, famous for its broasted chicken dinners and cold brews on tap.

www.elklakeresort.net
www.cultuslakeresort.com
www.crescentlakeresort.com

INDEX

ABOUT THE AUTHOR

Katy Bryce is a Bend-based free-lance writer and copywriter with a deep love for Oregon's mountains, deserts, and beaches. A Bend mountain biker since 1997, she has ridden every trail in the area and has volunteered for the Central Oregon Trail Alliance (COTA), building and maintaining trails. She and her husband, Chris, enjoy any traveling and adventures that include mountain biking, surfing, or eating tacos both in Oregon and all over the world. Learn more at www.katybryce.com.

Photo: *Abacus Photography*